I0221806

John Thomson

Descriptive Catalogue of the Series of Works Known as the Library of Old Authors

John Thomson

Descriptive Catalogue of the Series of Works Known as the Library of Old Authors

ISBN/EAN: 9783337219468

Printed in Europe, USA, Canada, Australia, Japan

Cover: Foto ©ninafisch / pixelio.de

More available books at **www.hansebooks.com**

BULLETIN

OF

THE FREE LIBRARY

OF PHILADELPHIA

NUMBER 2

DESCRIPTIVE CATALOGUE OF THE SERIES OF WORKS KNOWN AS THE LIBRARY OF OLD AUTHORS

BY

JOHN THOMSON

MARCH, 1899

COPYRIGHT, 1899,
BY
THE FREE LIBRARY OF PHILADELPHIA.

DESCRIPTIVE CATALOGUE

OF THE

SERIES OF WORKS KNOWN AS THE LIBRARY OF OLD AUTHORS

OF

The Free Library of Philadelphia

PREFACE

❧❧

T HE first BULLETIN of the Free Library comprised a descriptive catalogue of the writings of Sir Walter Scott.

The "Library of Old Authors," which is the subject of this present BULLETIN, contains a wealth of information capable of being appreciated by a large number of the general readers of Free Libraries. When the publisher of the "Library of Old Authors" entered upon the publication of the series now described, he was entering upon a comparatively new field. It may be that there are many valuable series of works which would be equally entitled with the present to be descriptively catalogued, but possibly they will not be found to contain such a variety of information from a bibliographical point of view as John Russell Smith's "Library of Old Authors." The catalogue now issued has been the result of much labour spread over a long period; and as the notes accumulated the writer felt that there was a quantity of material which would probably be of value to librarians and the frequenters of libraries.

The writer desires to express his thanks to Mr. Lorin Blodget, Jr., head of the Bindery and Public Documents Department in the Free Library, for his valuable assistance in the preparation of the index. It

3

is hoped that BULLETIN Number Three may be issued in June or July next. It will consist of an Index of first lines and of subjects of the poems of Robert Herrick. It is a trite remark that few persons ever find a quotation from Herrick, or desire to consult a particular poem of this popular poet, without realizing how much a complete index to his works is a necessity rather than a luxury. Several other BULLETINS are in a forward state, and will be issued as opportunity serves.

DESCRIPTIVE CATALOGUE

OF THE

SERIES OF WORKS KNOWN AS THE LIBRARY OF OLD AUTHORS

A Series of Rare Works COLLECTED AND PRINTED UNDER THE TITLE OF "LIBRARY OF OLD AUTHORS." London : John Russell Smith. 1856, etc. 61 vols. 8vo.

This series of works was undertaken by John Russell Smith and subsequently by Messrs. Reeves & Turner. The set under description comprises sixty-one volumes, and the works are described below alphabetically, under the name of the author. On Mr. Smith's retirement from business he sold this series to Mr. Reeves for £1000.

Ascham, Roger (circa 1515-1568).—THE WHOLE WORKS of Roger Ascham. Now first collected and revised. With a Life of the Author, by the Rev. Dr. Giles. 3 vols. bound in 4. 1864-65.

Dr. Giles states that the works of Ascham "have never been collected," and some polemical discourses, such as "Commentaries of Œcomenius," "Apologia pro "Cœna Dominica," and "Themata Theologica" have been omitted as unworthy of rescue from "merited oblivion." A "Life of Ascham" is given, vol. i. pt. 1, pp. ix.–c.

A REPORT | AND DISCOURSE written by | Roger Ascham, of the affaires | and state of Germany and the | Emperour Charles his Court, | duryng certaine yeares, | while the sayd Roger | was there. | At London. | ¶ Printed by Iohn Daye, | dwelling ouer Aldersgate. | Vol. iii., pp. 1-62.

Ascham was in Germany during the years 1550-52. Lowndes writes : " This ac-
" count is stated by Dr. Campbell to be one of the most delicate pieces of history that
" ever was penned in our language, evincing its author to have been a man as capa-
" ble of shining in the cabinet as in the closet."

GRANT'S ORATION ON THE LIFE AND DEATH OF ROGER ASCHAM.
Vol. iii., pp. 294–355.

This was first published by Ed. G[rant], 1578, as an introduction to his first edition of the " Letters." It is very bombastic in its style, but forms a great guide to the " facts and dates of Ascham's life." Grant was a friend both of Roger Ascham and of Camden, and for twenty years held the office of head master of Westminster School.

LATIN POEMS. Vol. iii., pp. 277–293.

LETTERS. Vol. i., pp. 1–458 ; and Vol. ii., pp. 1–196.

Volumes i. and ii. contain Ascham's " Letters." They enable the reader to trace the " chief facts of his life from the year 1539, when he was in full reputation as a " scholar at the University of Cambridge, to his death." To each of the letters, which are chiefly in Latin, the editor has prefixed a brief summary of its contents.

Forty of the two hundred and ninety-five letters were given to the public in this edition for the first time.

A list of the names of Ascham's correspondents, " alphabetically arranged," is given, vol. i. pt. i. pp. cxvii.–cxxi. ; and at the end of vol. i. pt. ii., and of vol. ii. p. 194, are given glossaries of the old words used in Ascham's letters.

SEVEN LETTERS OF GILES ASCHAM, Roger Ascham's Son, to the
Lord Treasurer, Burleigh. Vol. iii., pp. 356–365.

In Fuller's Worthies, the author wrote of Ascham that " he was an honest man "and could shoot. His ' Toxophilus' is a good book for young men, his ' School-"' master' for old men, his ' Epistles' for all men." In 1548 Ascham was tutor to the Princess Elizabeth, and afterwards ambassador's secretary to the Court of Charles V., and later he was secretary to King Edward VI. and to Queen Mary. After Mary's death, Queen Elizabeth retained him at court in the double capacity of secretary and tutor. This queen economically paid him only £20 a year by way of salary, though on his death she " declared that she would rather have lost £10,000 than her tutor " Ascham."

THE | SCHOLEMASTER | Or plaine and perfite way of teachyng | children, to understand, write, and speake, the | Latin tong, but specially purposed for the | private brynging up of youth in Jentlemen | and Noble mens houses, and commodious also | for all such, as have forgot the Latin tonge, | and would, by themselves, without a | Scholemaster, in short tyme, and | with small paines, recover | a sufficient habilitie, to | understand, write, | and speake | Latin. | ¶ By Roger Ascham. | ¶ An. 1570. | At London. | Printed by John Daye, dwelling | over Aldersgate. | ¶ Cum Gratia & Privilegio Regiæ Majestatis | per Decennium. | Vol. iii., pp. 63–276.

An interesting account is given by Ascham in the "Preface to the Reader" (pp. 78–87) of how this work originated.

The work is divided into two books. In the first Ascham sets out two stages of his method of learning Latin, and after a discussion of Plato's "plain notes to choose "a good wit in a child for learning," the writer closes with a severe attack on the "Italianated" Englishmen of the period, and in the second book he gives the third and fourth stages of his methods, with criticisms on Latin authors and remarks on various English writers.

TOXOPHILVS, | The schole of shootinge, | conteyned in two | bookes. | Vol. ii., after the "Letters" (new pagination), pp. 1–168.

The text in this volume is that of the first edition, which was printed in 4to, London, 1545. It has been many times reprinted. A glossary of "old words" in the Toxophilus is given at the end of the volume, pp. 166–167.

This work was dedicated to King Henry VIII. (see Letters xxxii. and xxxiv., etc., vol. i. pp. 77–81), in the hope of obtaining a pension to enable Ascham to make the tour of Italy, in which he was successful, receiving an annual pension of £10. On this work *see* "Retrospective Review," vol. iv. pp. 76–87.

One main object of Ascham in writing his "Toxophilus" was to present the public with a specimen of a purer and more correct English style than that to which they had been hitherto accustomed, and with the hope of calling the attention of the learned from the exclusive study of Greek and Latin to the cultivation of their vernacular language. The result which he contemplated was attained, and from the period of this publication the shackles of Latinity were broken, and composition in English prose became the object of eager and successful attention.

The whole work is a dialogue between Toxophilus, a lover of archery, and Philologus, a student. Toxophilus is Ascham himself, and Philologus is Sir John Cheke, the public orator of the university, celebrated for introducing into English schools the method (for two centuries pursued in England) of pronouncing Greek after English pronunciation, as distinguished from Italian pronunciation used throughout the remainder of Europe.

A series of verses, dedications, etc., from the various preceding editions, is given vol. i. pp. ci.–cxvi.

Aubrey, John (1626–1697).—MISCELLANIES UPON VARIOUS SUBJECTS. . . . To which is added Hydriotaphia; or, Urn-Burial, by Sir Thomas Browne. 1890.

Aubrey was a man best described as nobody's enemy but his own. He has left (see pp. x.–xiv.) some interesting memoranda of his "accidents" in life. He had "several love and lawe suites," lost all his fortune in litigation, never obtained a wife, but from the day he lost everything "enjoyed a happy delitescency," intermingled with "danger of arrests" and various chances of being killed. He was a friend of Anthony Wood, but the two men fell out, and Wood, while using a mass of information supplied by Aubrey for the former's two great works, described Aubrey some years later as "a shiftless person, roving and magotie-headed, and sometimes

"little better than erased." Notwithstanding this ill report, the fact is that Aubrey was a diligent antiquary, and his testimony is worthy of attention. Toland asserts of him that "though he was extremely superstitious, or seemed to be so, yet he was "a very honest man and most accurate in his account of matters of fact."

A horoscope of John Aubrey's nativity, from his own sketch, is given p. 222.

His miscellanies are on the following subjects:

	Page
1. Apparitions	70
2. Blows Invisible	119
3. Converse with Angels and Spirits	159
4. Corps-Candles in Wales	165

This is part of a letter from Aubrey to Mr. Baxter.

5. Day-Fatality of Rome	21

This was written by Dr. John Pell, who gave it to Aubrey.

6. Day-Fatality; or, Some Observations of Days Lucky and Unlucky	1
7. Dreams	49
8. Ecstacy	169
9. Fatalities of Families and Places	25
10. Glances of Love and Malice	172
11. Impulses	112
12. Knockings	117
13. Magick	130
14. Miranda	124
15. Omens	38
16. Oracles	168
17. Ostenta, or Portents	33
18. Predictions, etc.; Farther Additaments	196

These are by Mr. T. Stanley, translated from the "Various History of "Ælian."

19. Prophesies	120
20. Second-Sight, Additaments of	194
21. Second-Sighted Men in Scotland, An Accurate Account of	174

This section consists of two letters from "a learned friend" of Aubrey's in Scotland.

22. Transportation by an Invisible Power	142

This is a letter to Aubrey from Rev. Dr. Paschal, rector of Chedzoy, in Somersetshire.

23. Visions in a Beryl or Crystal	154
24. Visions without a Glass or Crystal	158
25. Voices	106

Browne, Sir Thomas (1605–1682). — HYDRIOTAPHIA. Urn-Burial; or, A Discourse of the Sepulchral Urns lately found in Norfolk.

This work is bound up in this series of books with Aubrey's "Miscellanies." Sir Thomas Browne, in his Religio Medici, had expressed some remarkable views as to women and marriage, so that when a few years later he married, lived happily, and had ten children, he was not altogether unfairly subjected to a good deal of raillery. His opinions included the thoughts that the "whole world was made for man, "but only the twelfth part of man for woman," and that "man is the whole world, "but woman only the rib or crooked part of man."

In "Hydriotaphia," the author, having accidentally discovered a few urns at Walsingham, proceeds to discuss with great learning the burial customs that have existed in different countries at various times. This work, originally published in 1658, had reached a sixth edition by 1686.

BRAMPTON URNS. Particulars of some Urns found in Brampton Field, February, 1667–8. Corrected from three MS. copies in the British Museum and the Bodleian Library.

This is added to the "Hydriotaphia" (pp. 287–295), and was originally published in 1712.

Camden, William (1551–1623).—REMAINS | CONCERNING | BRITAIN: | Their |

Languages,	Impresses,
Names,	Apparel,
Surnames,	Artillerie,
Allusions,	Wise Speeches,
Anagramms,	Proverbs,
Armories,	Poesies,
Moneys,	Epitaphs.

Written by William Camden | Esquire, [with Portrait.] Clarenceux, King of Arms, | Surnamed the Learned. | The Seventh Impression, much amended, | with many rare Antiquities never before | Imprinted. | By the Industry and Care of John Philipot | Somerset Herald: and W. D. Gent. | London, | Printed for, and sold by, Charles Harper, at the | Flower de Luce over against St. Dunstan's Church, and | John Amery at the Peacock over against Fetter Lane, | both in Fleetstreet, 1674. |

Camden's remarkable work, the "Britannia," which was "an honour to its author "and the glory of his country," was first published in Latin in 1586, and seven

editions were issued in the author's lifetime. The first translation into English was made in the year 1611.

It must be remembered that when Camden entered on his task topography was a new science. The fourth edition (1594) was the cause of the literary "terrific com-"bat" between Ralph Brooke and Camden. Brooke pointed out certain errors in Camden. How Camden in the fifth edition (1600) superciliously repudiated the charge of having fallen into error, while at the same time he adopted Brooke's "corrigenda," is the subject of one of Disraeli's interesting chapters. (*See* "Calami-"ties," vol. ii. pp. 343-356.)

The "Remains Concerning Britain," founded on "Britannia," was published under the initials of M. N., the last letters of Willia*M* Camde*N*, in 1605.

The work itself is very interesting,—*e.g.*, the "rebuses" (p. 179), where an amorous youth, who courted a damsel named Rose Hill, painted a rose, a hill, an eye, a loaf, and a well, meaning, if you will spell it, "Rose Hill I love well."

So are the anagrams, as that (p. 184) on Mary Queen of Scots,—"Maria Ste-"varta,"—which will read "Veritas armata."

At pp. 316-336 are given a series of proverbs which "doubtless suggested John "Ray's celebrated work" or "collection" of proverbs. The chapter on epigrams is capital, but is excelled in amusement by the selection of epitaphs (pp. 386-440), of which those (p. 417) on Dr. Caius (1510-1573), the founder of Caius College, Cambridge, "Fui caius," and on the learned Julius Scaliger (1484-1558), "Scaligeri "quod reliquum," are pithy and pertinent, but inferior to that (p. 434) on a shrew:

> "We lived one and twenty year
> "As man and wife together;
> "I could not stay her longer here,
> "She's gone I know not whither;
> "But did I know, I do protest
> "(I speak it not to flatter)
> "Of all the women in the world,
> "I swear I'd ne're come at her.
> "Her body is bestowed well,
> "This handsome grave doth hide her,
> "And sure her soul is not in hell,
> "The divel could ne're abide her:
> "But I suppose she's soar'd aloft,
> "For in the late great thunder,
> "Me thought I heard her very voice,
> "Rending the clowds asunder."

The celebrated "Camden Society" (founded 1838) was named after this anti-quary.

These "Remains" are the "rude rubble and outcast rubbish," as he calls it, of his more serious work, "Britannia." The "Britannia" cost him ten years' toil. Nothing of the kind had been produced between it and Leland's "Itinerary." Camden's "Britannia" was an enlargement and improvement of Leland's book.

Carew, Thomas (1598–1639).—THE POEMS AND MASQUE of Thomas Carew, Gentleman of the Privy-Chamber to King Charles I. and Cup-Bearer to His Majesty. With an Introductory Memoir, an Appendix of Unauthenticated Poems from MSS., Notes, and a Table of First Lines. Edited by Joseph Woodfall Ebsworth. 1893.

The dates of this poet's birth and death are disputed. The editor of this edition attributes his death to the year 1638. There is an Introductory Memoir, pp. ix.–xxv.

Page

BIBLIOGRAPHY OF THOMAS CAREW 260

CŒLVM BRITANNICVM. A MASQUE 129

This was performed at White Hall, in the Banquetting-House, on Shrove Tuesday Night, the 18 of February, 1633. The inventors of the masque were Carew and Inigo Jones. Henry Lawes, the celebrated musician of that day, set the songs and dialogues in the play to apt tunes. This was at one time attributed to Davenant. Pope not only admired Carew, but copied him in various places.

Suckling, in his "Session of the Poets," charges Carew with overpolishing his lines:

" His muse was hide-bound and the issue of 's brain
" Was seldome brought forth but with labour and pain."

EXTRA POEMS FROM MANUSCRIPTS 169

These are "more or less doubtful, or authenticated."

PARAPHRASE, A, OF CERTAIN PSALMS 191

These have given rise to much unpleasant comment. They are only copies of rough drafts, not corrected by the author. The editor takes the opportunity of roundly denouncing the article on Carew in the Dictionary of National Biography, by Dr. Augustus Jessopp, who rakes up various stories of Carew not better founded than "it looks as if his life had been short- "ened by irregular habits," and bits of gossip from Hales, of Eton (called the early Socinian Canon of Windsor), who, if he is correct in his statements, knew his facts only under the seal of confession, and, by revealing them to a woman who hated Carew, placed himself beneath contempt. It is just that Dr. Ebsworth should condemn the criticisms of such a confessor and his ecclesiastical biographer who founds his statements on Hales's revelations. (*See* p. 252.)

POEMS 1

Chapman, George (1559–1634).—HOMER'S BATRACHOMYOMACHIA, HYMNS, AND EPIGRAMS. Hesiod's Works and Days. Musæus' Hero and Leander. Juvenal's Fifth Satire. Translated by

George Chapman. With Introduction and Notes by the Rev. Richard Hooper. To which is added a Glossarial Index to the whole of Chapman's Classical Translations. 1888.

This volume makes, with the Iliad and Odyssey, a translation of the " whole of " the works ascribed to Homer."

Page

BATRACHOMYOMACHIA, THE 1

The " Batrachomyomachia; or, the Battaile of Frogs and Mise," is entitled by Chapman " the Crowne of all Homer's Workes." It was first published in 1624. When the great poet found that his Iliad and Odyssey were lightly regarded, he " writ in contempt of men this ridiculous poem " of vermin, giving them nobility of birth, valorous elocution not inferior " to his heroes."

EPIGRAMS, CERTAIN, AND OTHER POEMS 122

GLOSSARIAL INDEX 257

HESIOD. The Book of Days 201

This is an interesting anticipation of many volumes written centuries later on fatality days, and lucky and unlucky days.

HESIOD: THE GEORGICS OF 137

Hesiod was a Greek poet, born at Ascra, in Bœotia. His " Works and " Days" gave the idea of the Georgics to Virgil. A copy of this translation is very rare, and Mr. Hooper did a good service in printing this excellent edition. Hesiod was probably contemporary with Homer, although many think he preceded Homer by at least thirty years. Chapman's version was followed by translations by Thomas Cooke in 1728 and 1740. Cooke was pilloried by Pope in the Dunciad.

HYMNS OF HOMER, ALL THE 18

JUVENAL. A Just Reproofe of a Romane Smell-Feast: Being the Fifth Satyre of Juvenal 237

This satire was apparently purposed to be only one of several translations by Chapman, but it was the only one he printed. It was appended to a tract published in 1629, and entitled: " A Justification of a Strange action " of Nero in burying with a solemne Funerall one of the cast hayres of his " Mistress Poppæa." Mr. Hooper did not consider the tract worth reprinting, but the extract from Juvenal was given to complete " Chapman's Clas- " sical Translations."

MUSÆUS, THE DIVINE POEM OF 207

The " Hero and Leander" of Musæus, translated by Chapman, is " per- " haps one of the rarest books in the whole range of English literature." A copy in the Bodleian is supposed to be unique. It is a curious little volume about two inches high and one inch broad. The first two lines, for instance, owing to the smallness of the volume, are broken up. When printed in full lines they read thus:

" Goddess, relate the witness-bearing light
" Of Loves, that would not bear a human sight;
" The Sea-man that transported marriages,
" Shipt in the night, his bosom plowing th' seas."

They were printed in the Bodleian copy in this wise:

" Goddess, relate
" The witnesse-bearing light
" Of loves, that would not beare
" A human sight.

" The sea-man
" That transported marriages,
" Shipt in the night,
" His bosom ploughing the seas."

Chapman, George.—The ILIADS OF HOMER, Prince of Poets, never before in any Language truly Translated, with a Comment on some of his Chief Places. Done according to the Greek. With Introduction and Notes by the Rev. Richard Hooper. 2 vols. 1888.

It is not the place here to comment on whether Homer wrote or only collected and put into shape the poems known as his. George Chapman, as a poet, was cleverly described as " a rough nut externally, but one who contains a most sweet kernel." His translation of Homer has been variously esteemed. It is in rhymed verse of fourteen syllables. The last twelve books were translated in less than fifteen weeks. His Homer is generally admitted to be " one of the great achievements of the Eli-" zabethan age, a monument of skill and devotion." Daniel, Ben Jonson, Waller, Pope, Coleridge, and Lamb have all paid tribute to the energy and force of this translation. No one denies that it is a free translation, but Emerson, Swinburne, and notably Keats (in his well-known Sonnet) have all been enthusiastic admirers of Chapman's labours.

At the end of vol. ii. (pp. 277–302) are a series of twenty-two sonnets addressed to noble patrons. Fourteen of these appeared in the first folio edition of the Iliad. Sonnet xxi. is addressed to Robert Carr, Viscount Rochester, subsequently created Earl of Somerset.

The Iliad and Odyssey of Homer (says Chapman) were " worthily called the " ' Sun and Moon of the Earth.' "

Chapman, George.—The ODYSSEYS OF HOMER, Translated According to the Greek. With Introduction and Notes by the Rev. Richard Hooper. 2 vols. 1874.

Chapman's Odyssey was originally published in folio, 1614–16. Of this translation the edition now under description was, in 1857, the only edition besides that superintended by the author himself. Chapman adopted the ten-syllabled heroic

couplet for the Odyssey, and the greatest complaint concerning his translation is that he "too frequently wandered from the original, and not seldom curtailed passages." Of the main incidents of his life we have no record. "What he was," says Mr. Hooper, "where he lived, whether he was married, are all unknown to us." It has been maintained (*see* Minto) that Chapman was the rival poet referred to by Shakespeare in his Sonnets.

Crashaw, Richard (1613–1649).—THE COMPLETE WORKS of Richard Crashaw, Canon of Loretto. Edited by William B. Turnbull. 1858.

This seems to have been the first new edition of the whole of Crashaw's poems, and it has been succeeded by fuller and more complete versions, notably that by Dr. A. B. Grosart, published in 1872. The "fertility of Crashaw's imagination has "made him popular with succeeding poets." Milton in many passages of the Hymn to the Nativity and of Paradise Lost is indebted to Crashaw. Pope availed himself in his Epistle of Eloisa to Abelard of lines from Crashaw: and Coleridge says that Crashaw's poem on Saint Teresa (p. 67) inspired the second part of Christabel. (*See* Dictionary of National Biography.)

Drayton, Michael (1563–1631).—THE COMPLETE WORKS of Michael Drayton [with Portrait]. Now first collected. With Introductions and Notes by the Rev. Richard Hooper. 3 vols. 1876.

Only two works of this poet have been included in these volumes. The "Com-"plete Works" were intended to be comprised in from six to eight volumes, and a new memoir of Drayton was promised in the last volume. Only three volumes were issued in this edition.

(*a*) POLY-OLBION. A | Chorographicall | Description Of All | The Tracts, Rivers, | Movntains, Forests, | and other Parts of this Renowned | Isle of Great Britain, | With intermixture of the most Remarkable | Stories, Antiquities, Wonders, Rarities, Pleasures, | and Commodities of the same. | . . . | London, | Printed for Iohn Marriott, Iohn Grismand, | and Thomas Dewe. 1622. | Vols i., ii., and pp. 1–228 of vol. iii.

The title alone sufficiently indicates this as one of the most remarkable "poetical" efforts ever made. It is almost as if Drayton had issued a versification of Camden's "Britannia" or a work similar to one of Baedeker's Guide-Books. Ellis, in his "Specimens of the Early English Poets," says this is "certainly a wonderful work, "exhibiting at once the learning of an historian, an antiquary, a naturalist, and a "geographer, and embellished by the imagination of a poet." The first part, comprising eighteen "songs" or books of the Poly-Olbion, was published in 1613 and reprinted in 1622 with a second part. It consists of 15,092 lines in Alexandrine couplets divided into thirty "songs" or parts. The idea of a versified guide-book to England has been termed "eminently original." A "Table of the Chiefest "Passages in the Illustrations" [*i.e.*, "Notes"] is given vol. i. pp. xlvii.–liv.

(*b*) THE | HARMONIE | OF THE CHURCH, | containing | The Spiri-
tuall Songes and | holy Hymnes, of godly men, Patriarkes
and | Prophetes. . . . | Now (newlie) reduced into sundrie
kinds of | English Meeter : meete to be read or sung | . . . |
London | Printed by Richard Ihones | at the Rose and Crowne,
neere Holborne | Bridge, 1591. | Vol. iii., pp. 229–294.

This was Drayton's earliest publication, and was printed as " The Triumphes of
" the Church," but for some unexplained reason it gave offence, and the whole impres-
sion (excepting forty copies seized by the Archbishop of Canterbury) was destroyed
by public order. A unique copy of the suppressed volume, having, however, a different title-page, is in the British Museum. Many consider his " Song of Salomon"
(vol. iii. pp. 247–258) the best poetical part of this work. The whole is a metrical
rendering of portions of the Scriptures.

It is to be regretted that only these three volumes were issued, especially as the
poet's " Nymphidia" (an inspiration to Herrick), and Drayton's most lasting writing
as a composition, is not included.

Drummond, William (1585–1649).—THE POETICAL WORKS of
William Drummond of Hawthornden. Edited by William B.
Turnbull. 1890.

Drummond is described as " distinguished as the first Scottish poet who wrote
" well in English." Hallam and Hazlitt have both written highly in commendation
of his sonnets. There is one piece at the end of the volume which is attributed to
Drummond, but as to the authorship of which doubt must always exist. It is unlike
anything else he wrote, and was not published till 1691. It is entitled " Polemo-
" Middinia," or the battle of the dunghill. It has the appearance of being a part of
a larger poem, and alludes to some rustic dispute which was probably a matter of
considerable local notoriety. The facts seem unknown now. It is the first macaronic poem by a native of Great Britain, and the burlesque verse with the inter-
mingling of English with Latin words and the contortions of the English by the use
of Latin terminations and Latin constructions, is very clever and amusing.

The author was a firm royalist in principles, and kept as clear as he could of the
risks and troubles of the civil war, but did not long survive the murder of Charles I.,
his own life being shortened by grief for the death of his sovereign. Drayton and
Ben Jonson were among his friends.

His writings brought him into trouble with the revolutionary party, and they com-
pelled him to furnish a quota of men to fight against the cause he had espoused.
He had estates in three counties, and could not be called on for whole men, but
fractions from each county. He wrote to the king :

" Of all these forces raised against the king
" 'Tis my strange hap not one whole man to bring
" From divers parishes, yet divers men,
" But all in halfs and quarters : great king, then,
" In halfs and quarters if they come 'gainst thee,
" In halfs and quarters send them back to me."

Hazlitt, W. Carew (1834–   ).—EARLY POPULAR POETRY OF
SCOTLAND AND THE NORTHERN BORDER. Edited by David
Laing, LL.D., in 1822 and 1826. Rearranged and Revised
with Additions and a Glossary. 2 vols. 1895.

This is to some extent an amalgamation of two works published by Dr. Laing in
1822 and 1826, entitled " Select Remains of Ancient Popular Poetry in Scotland"
and " Early Metrical Tales."

The poems, etc., included in this series are given below in alphabetical order:

	Vol.	Page
ADAM BEL, CLYM OF THE CLEUGH, AND WILLIAM OF CLOWDESLÈ	II.	90
ADVERTISEMENTS PREFIXED TO FORMER EDITIONS	I.	xiii.
ALLANE-A'-MAUT, ANE BALLAT OF :	II.	60
ARTHURE, THE AWNTYRS OFF, AT THE TERNE WATHELYN	I.	1
AUCHTERMUCHTY, THE WYF OF	II.	47
AWNTYRS OFF ARTHURE AT THE TERNE WATHELYN, THE	I.	1
BALLAT OF ALLANE-A'-MAUT, ANE	II.	60
BALLAT OF MATRYMONIE, ANE	II.	74
BALLET OF THE NINE NOBLES, ANE	I.	300
BALLET SHEWING HOW A DUMB WYFF WAS MAID TO SPEIK, A	II.	28
BATTLE OF HARLAW, THE	I.	116
BERDOK, KING	II.	21
CLYM OF THE CLEUGH, ADAM BEL, AND WILLIAM OF CLOWDESLÈ	II.	90
COLKELBIE SOW, THE TALE OF	I.	179
CURSING, SIR JOHN ROWLL'S	I.	289
DESCRIPTIOUN OF PEDDER COFFEIS, ANE	II.	67
DREAME, ANE GODLIE, COMPYLIT IN SCOTISH METER	II.	279
DREME, LICHTOUN'S	II.	1
DUIK OF ORLYANCE IN DEFENCE OF THE SCOTS, THE	I.	304
EPISTILL OF THE HERMEIT OF ALAREIT TO THE GRAY FREIRS, THE	I.	175
ESTMERE, KING	II.	80
FERMORAR AND HIS DOCHTER, THE	I.	112
GAIST, THE LAYING OF LORD FERGUS'S	I.	284
GLASSINBERRY, A POEM BY	I.	307
GLOSSARY, INDEX OF PRINCIPAL MATTERS AND	II.	321
GODLIE DREAME, COMPYLIT IN SCOTISH METER, ANE	II.	279
GYRE-CARLING, THE	II.	18
HARLAW, THE BATTLE OF	I.	116
HERMEIT OF ALAREIT, THE EPISTILL OF THE, TO THE GRAY FREIRS	I.	175
HISTORY OF A LORD AND HIS THREE SONS, THE	II.	211
HISTORY OF SIR EGER, SIR GRYME, AND SIR GRAY STEILL, THE	II.	119
INDEX OF PRINCIPAL MATTERS AND GLOSSARY	II.	321
JOHN THE REEVE	I.	250
JOK AND JYNNY, THE WOWING OF	II.	24
KING BERDOK	II.	21

THE LIBRARY OF OLD AUTHORS

	Vol.	Page
KING ESTMERE	II.	80
KING JAMES THE SEXT, THE PROMINE TO	II.	268
KING ORFEO; ORFEO AND HEURODIS, OR	I.	59
LAYING OF LORD FERGUS'S GAIST, THE	I.	284
LICHTOUN'S DREME	II.	1
LILLIAN, ROSWALL AND	II.	239
LORD AND HIS THREE SONS, THE HISTORY OF A	II.	211
LOVERS QUARREL, THE; OR, ROSAMOND OF SCOTLAND	II.	302
MAIDIN, THE MURNING	II.	34
MANER OF THE CRYING OF ANE PLAYE, THE	II.	11
MATRYMONIE, ANE BALLAT OF	II.	74
MAY, WELCUM TO	II.	44
MURNING MAIDIN, THE	II.	34
NOBLES, ANE BALLET OF THE NINE	I.	300
ORFEO AND HEURODIS; OR, KING ORFEO	I.	59
ORLYANCE, THE DUIK OF, IN DEFENCE OF THE SCOTS	I.	304
PEDDER COFFEIS, ANE DESCRIPTIOUN OF	II.	67
PLAYE, THE MANER OF THE CRYING OF ANE	II.	11
POEM BY GLASSINBERRY, A	I.	307
PREFACE	I.	vii.
PRIESTS OF PEBLIS, THE THRIE TAILES OF THE THRIE	I.	127
PROMINE TO KING JAMES THE SEXT, THE	II.	268
PYSTYL OF SWETE SUSAN, THE	I.	43
QUENE OF ELF-LAND; THOMAS OF ERSYLDOUNE AND THE	I.	81
RAUF COILZEAR, THE TALE OF	I.	212
REEVE, JOHN THE	I.	250
RING OF THE ROY ROBERT, THE	I.	313
ROSAMOND OF SCOTLAND; THE LOVERS QUARREL; OR	II.	302
ROSWALL AND LILLIAN	II.	239
ROY ROBERT, THE RING OF THE	I.	313
SCOTS, THE DUIK OF ORLYANCE IN DEFENCE OF THE	I.	304
SIR EGER, SIR GRYME, AND SIR GRAY STEILL, THE HISTORY OF	II.	119
SIR JOHN BARLEYCORN	II.	64
SIR JOHN ROWLL'S CURSING	I.	289
SOW, THE TALE OF COLKELBIE.	I.	179
SWETE SUSAN, THE PYSTYL OF	I.	43
SYMMIE AND HIS BRUTHER	II.	5
TALE OF COLKELBIE SOW, THE	I.	179
TALE OF RAUF COILZEAR, THE	I.	212
TAYIS BANK	I.	169
TERNE WATHELYN, THE AWNTYRS OFF ARTHURE AT THE	I.	1
THOMAS OF ERSYLDOUNE AND THE QUENE OF ELF-LAND	I.	81
THRIE TAILES OF THE THRIE PRIESTS OF PEBLIS, THE	I.	127
WELCUM TO MAY	II.	44
WILLIAM OF CLOWDESLÈ, ADAM BEL, AND CLYM OF THE CLEUGH	II.	90
WOWING OF JOK AND JYNNY, THE	II.	24

	Vol.	Page
WYFF, A BALLET SHEWING HOW A DUMB WYFF WAS MAID TO SPEIK	II.	28
WYF OF AUCHTERMUCHTY, THE	II.	47

At the end of vol. ii. (pp. 323-343) is given an Index of Principal Matters and Glossary.

Hazlitt, W. Carew.—REMAINS OF THE EARLY POPULAR POETRY OF ENGLAND. Collected and Edited, With Introductions and Notes. 4 vols. 1864-66.

These volumes contain a collection of sixty pieces, including "all Ritson's vol-"ume (published 1791) of 'Pieces of Ancient Popular Poetry,'" and pieces from the collections of Hartshorne, Utterson, and Halliwell. There are sixteen fac-similes of title-pages to some of the old pieces, of which that to "Tom Thumbe" is to be found in vol. ii. p. 175, and lists of the other fifteen are given in vols. iii. and iv. respectively after the "Contents."

In vol. i. p. 153, is reprinted "The Commonyng of Ser John Mandevelle and the "gret Souden," a curious attempt "to versify one of the most popular books of its "kind,—The Voiage and Travaile of Sir John Maundeville, Kt." Whether more than a few extracts from Maundeville were so treated is not known.

Mr. Hazlitt states that the versions of "Adam Bel" and "Tom Thumbe," etc., have been much corrected from the versions given by Ritson. Of course, readers will prefer, where possible, to refer to Francis James Child's "English and Scottish "Ballads" for these ballads and their variations.

In vol. i. are given some interesting pieces,—e.g., "The Lyfe of Roberte the "Deuyll" (p. 217) and "Kynge Roberd of Cysille" (p. 264), showing how the history of Robert of Sicily has become embellished by circumstances taken from the Life of Robert the Devil.

Nearly every piece is preceded by a useful bibliographical note, tracing the origin and various editions of each poem.

The pieces included in these four volumes are given below in alphabetical order:

	Vol.	Page
ADAM BEL, CLYM OF THE CLOUGHE, AND WYLLYAM OF CLOUDESLE	II.	131
ARMONYE OF BYRDES, THE	III.	184
BACONS BRAZEN-HEADS PROPHESIE, A PIECE OF FRIAR	IV.	263
BASYN, THE TALE OF THE	III.	42
BATAYLE OF EGYNGECOURTE, THE	II.	88
BIRTH, LIFE, DEATH, WIL, AND EPITAPH OF JACK PUFFE, GENTLE-MAN, THE	IV.	311
BOKE OF MAYD EMLYN, THE	IV.	81
BOOKE IN MEETER OF ROBIN CONSCIENCE, THE	III.	221
BYRDES, THE ARMONYE OF	III.	184
BYRDES, THE PARLAMENT OF	III.	164
CARPENTERS TOOLS, THE DEBATE OF THE	I.	79
CHILDE OF BRISTOWE, THE	I.	110

	Vol.	Page
CLYM OF THE CLOUGHE : *see* ADAM BEL	II.	131
COKWOLDS DAUNCE, THE	I.	35
COLYN BLOWBOLS TESTAMENT	I.	91
COMMONYNG OF SER JOHN MANDEVELLE AND THE GRET SOUDEN, THE	I.	153
CUPIDS TRIUMPH; THE LOVERS QUARREL, OR	II.	251
DANE HEW, MUNK OF LEICESTRE, A MERY JEST OF.	III.	130
DEBATE AND STRYFE BETWENE SOMER AND WYNTER, THE	III.	29
DEBATE OF THE CARPENTERS TOOLS, THE	I.	79
DOCTOUR DOUBBLE ALE	III.	297
EGYNGECOURTE, THE BATAYLE OF	II.	88
FAIR LADY OF FAGUELL, THE KNIGHT OF CURTESY AND THE	II.	65
FRERE AND THE BOYE, A MERY GESTE OF THE	III.	54
GALAUNT, A TREATISE OF A.	III.	147
GLASSE TO VIEWE THE PRIDE OF VAINE GLORIOUS WOMEN, A	IV.	245
HISTORY OF TOM THUMB, THE	II.	193
HOW A MERCHANDE DYD HYS WYFE BETRAY	I.	193
HOW A SERGEAUNT WOLDE LERNE TO BE A FRERE, A MERY JEST	III.	119
HOW THE GOODE WIF THAUGHT HIR DOUGHTER..	I.	178
HOW THE PLOWMAN LERNED HIS PATER NOSTER, A MERY GESTE	I.	209
HOW THE WISE MAN TAUGHT HIS SON	I.	168
HYE WAY TO THE SPYTTEL HOUS, THE	IV.	17
JACK PUFFE, GENTLEMAN, THE BIRTH, LIFE, DEATH, WIL, AND EPITAPH OF	IV.	311
JOHN BON AND MAST PERSON	IV.	1
JUSTES OF THE MONETHS OF MAY AND JUNE, THE.	II.	109
KING AND A POORE NORTHERNE MAN, THE	IV.	290
KING AND THE BARKER, THE	I.	1
KNIGHT OF CURTESY, THE, AND THE FAIR LADY OF FAGUELL	II.	65
KNYGHT AND HIS WYFE, THE	II.	16
KYNG AND THE HERMYT, THE	I.	11
KYNGE ROBERD OF CYSILLE	I.	264
LONDON STONE AND THE FAYRE PUSELL THE BOSSE OF BYLLYNGESGATE, THE MARYAGE OF	III.	161
LOVERS QUARREL, THE; OR, CUPIDS TRIUMPH	II.	251
LYFE OF ROBERTE THE DEUYLL, THE	I.	217
MARYAGE OF LONDON STONE AND THE FAYRE PUSELL THE BOSSE OF BYLLYNGESGATE, THE.	III.	161
MARYAGE, THE PAYNE AND SOROWE OF EVYLL	IV.	73
MAY AND JUNE, THE JUSTES OF THE MONETHS OF	II.	109
MAYD EMLYN, THE BOKE OF	IV.	81
MERCHANT AND HIS SON, THE	I.	132
MERRY IESTE OF A SHREWDE AND CURSTE WYFE LAPPED IN MORRELLES SKIN, A	IV.	179
MERY GESTE, HOW THE PLOWMAN LERNED HIS PATER NOSTER, A	I.	209
MERY GESTE OF THE FRERE AND THE BOYE, A	III.	54

	Vol.	Page
MERY JEST HOW A SERGEAUNT WOLDE LERNE TO BE A FRERE, A .	III.	119
MERY JEST OF DANE HEW, MUNK OF LEICESTRE, A	III.	130
MERY JEST OF THE MYLNER OF ABYNGTON, A	III.	98
MYLNER OF ABYNGTON, A MERY JEST OF THE	III.	98
NEW NUTBORUNE MAYD UPON THE PASSION OF CRYSTE, THE .	III.	1
NOTBROWNE MAYDE, THE	II.	271
NUTBORUNE MAYD, THE NEW, UPON THE PASSION OF CRYSTE .	III.	1
PARLAMENT OF BYRDES, THE.	III.	164
PATER NOSTER, PROUDE WYUES	IV.	147
PAYNE AND SOROWE OF EVYLL MARYAGE, THE	IV.	73
PIECE OF FRIAR BACONS BRAZEN-HEADS PROPHESIE, A . . .	IV.	263
PIERS OF FULLHAM	II.	1
PORE HELPE, A	III.	249
PROUDE WYUES PATER NOSTER	IV.	147
RAGMAN ROLL	I.	68
ROBERTE THE DEUYLL, THE LYFE OF	I.	217
ROBIN CONSCIENCE, THE BOOKE IN MEETER OF	III.	221
SCHOLE-HOUSE OF WOMEN, THE.	IV.	97
SER JOHN MANDEVELLE AND THE GRET SOUDEN, THE COMMONYNG OF	I.	153
SHREWDE AND CURSTE WYFE LAPPED IN MORRELLES SKIN, A MERY IESTE OF A	IV.	179
SMYTH AND HIS DAME, THE	III.	200
SOMER AND WYNTER, THE DEBATE AND STRYFE BETWENE . . .	III.	29
SPYTTEL HOUS, THE HYE WAY TO THE	IV.	17
SQUYR OF LOWE DEGRE, THE	II.	21
STANS PUER AD MENSAM	III.	23
SYR PENY	I.	159
TALE OF THE BASYN, THE	III.	42
TESTAMENT, COLYN BLOWBOLS	I.	91
THRUSH AND THE NIGHTINGALE, THE.	I.	50
TOM THUMB, THE HISTORY OF	II.	193
TOM THUMBE, HIS LIFE AND DEATH	II.	167
TOTENHAM, THE TURNAMENT OF.	III.	82
TREATISE OF A GALAUNT, A	III.	147
TREATYSE SHEWING AND DECLARING THE PRYDE AND ABUSE OF WOMEN NOW A DAYES, A	IV.	227
TURNAMENT OF TOTENHAM, THE.	III.	82
VOX AND THE WOLF, OF THE	I.	58
VOX POPULI VOX DEI	III.	267
WELCH TRAVELLER, THE	IV.	321
WOMEN, A GLASSE TO VIEWE THE PRIDE OF VAINE GLORIOUS .	IV.	245
WOMEN NOW A DAYES, A TREATYSE SHEWING AND DECLARING THE PRYDE AND ABUSE OF	IV.	227
WOMEN, THE SCHOLE-HOUSE OF	IV.	97
WYLLYAM OF CLOUDESLÈ, ADAM BEL, CLYM OF THE CLOUGHE, AND .	II.	131

Hearne, Thomas (1678-1735).—RELIQUIÆ HEARNIANÆ: The Remains of Thomas Hearne, M.A., of Edmund Hall [with Portrait]. Being Extracts from his MS. Diaries, Collected, with a few Notes, by Philip Bliss. Second Edition, Enlarged. 3 vols. 1869. Index, 2 col., vol. iii. pp. 319–358.

These remains of this celebrated antiquary are "derived from one hundred and "forty-five small 8vo manuscript volumes, one of which the writer was accustomed "to carry constantly in his pocket . . . in order to note down what he thought, what "he read, what he saw himself, or what he was told by others." The volumes date from July 4, 1705, to June 4, 1735, six days before his death. Mr. Russell Smith states that this edition includes nearly twice the number of selections from Hearne's Diaries that were included in Dr. Bliss's first edition. The book is a curious mixture of lengthy extracts from the works he read or which came under his notice, criticism, gossip about his friends and enemies, public matters, Oxford life, and, indeed, anything that interested him. It is made valuable by the addition of an admirable index. The accounts of Sally Salisbury, vol. ii. pp. 159, 192, and 209, "The Whipping Stories," vol. ii. p. 260, and vol. iii. p. 270, and Hearne's "Obser- "vations on Pope," especially those about Theobald (vol. iii. pp. 137, 142, and 167), are good illustrations of the character of this work.

In the Appendixes should be noted the collection of "Graces" (vol. iii. pp. 217–230) at nineteen of the colleges at Oxford, and the "Bibliotheca Hearniana" (vol. iii. pp. 272–318), being "Excerpts from the Catalogue" of Hearne's library, which gives an interesting list of the more important books collected by this bibliomaniac. Hearne compiled and edited forty-one works, and there is an amusing note upon him in Dibdin's "Bibliomania," pp. 333–336. A list of thirty-seven of his works is given in the Dictionary of National Biography, vol. xxv. p. 337.

Gibbon (*see* his "Posthumous Works," vol. ii. p. 711) sneers at Hearne somewhat severely, and, it is thought, very unjustly, and Pope pilloried him in the Dunciad (book iii. lines 185–190) as "Wormius" in the lines:

> "But who is he, in closet close y-pent,
> "Of sober face, with learned dust besprent?
> "Right well mine eyes arede the myster wight,
> "On parchment scraps y-fed and Wormius hight.
> "To future ages may thy dulness last,
> "As thou preserv'st the dulness of the past!"

Hearne's editions of many of the old English chronicles were the only ones that existed till the recent publication of the Rolls Series of historical works, and of some, his are still the only editions in print.

He was appointed to a post in the Bodleian library in 1701, and in 1712 became second keeper of that institution.

Herrick, Robert (1591–1674).—HESPERIDES : The Poems and other Remains of Robert Herrick [with Portrait]. Edited by W. Carew Hazlitt. 2 vols. 1890.

The " Hesperides" was first published in 1648, when Herrick was fifty-seven years old. Hallam (*see* " Literature of Europe") gives a flattering review of this poet's writings.

The " Memoir" is given vol. i. pp. vii.–xxxv. It is enlarged and revised from the " Biographical Notice" by Mr. S. W. S[inger], published in 1846 (*see* British Poets).

The " Hesperides" is reprinted from the edition of 1648, and gives the poems as presented by the author to the public. The "Noble Numbers" is reprinted from the edition of 1647.

After the " Biographical Notice" are printed (vol. i. pp. xxxvi.–xlix.) fourteen letters written by the poet to his uncle, Sir William Herrick, between 1613 and 1617. They are principally applications for money.

Some poems which Mr. Hazlitt in earlier editions claimed as Herrick's and which were included in the Appendix of the edition published in 1869 are withdrawn in the edition under description. They " can clearly be shown to belong to other " writers." Herrick is memorable for his descriptions of old English country life, in its wakes, wassails, sports of Christmas-tide and Twelfth-Night, the May-day games and harvest home romps.

Hesiod.—BOOK OF DAYS. (*See* Chapman.)

Hesiod.—GEORGICS. (*See* Chapman.)

Homer.—BATRACHOMYOMACHIA ; or, The Battaile of Frogs and Mise. (*See* Chapman.)

Homer.—ILIADS. (*See* Chapman.)

Homer.—ODYSSEYS. (*See* Chapman.)

Juvenal.—FIFTH SATIRE. (*See* Chapman.)

Langland, William (1330–1400).—THE VISION AND CREED OF PIERS PLOUGHMAN. Edited from a contemporary manuscript, with a historical Introduction, Notes, and a Glossary. By Thomas Wright. 2 vols. 1887.

	Vol.	Page
CREED, THE, OF PIERS PLOUGHMAN	II.	449

Professor J. W. Hales, a contributor to the Dictionary of National Biography, believes this to be by a different author from the author of the " Vision," and believes it to have been written about 1394, the date of the persecution of Walter Brute, at Hereford. The " Creed" was written by one who approved the opinions of Wycliffe. The " Vision" attacked the Church and State. The " Creed" was confined to the Church.

	Vol.	Page
VISION, THE, OF PIERS PLOUGHMAN	I.	1

It has not been yet ascertained with certainty by whom this satire was written, but it is generally (and apparently correctly) attributed to a William Langland, Langeland, or Longland. Bishop Bale, of Ossory, in the sixteenth century, credited one Robert Langland, a priest, of Shropshire, with the authorship, as also did Crowley, its earliest editor, in 1550. Internal evidence is conclusive that the writer was associated with the western midlands, as he particularly connects his "Vision" with the Malvern Hills. It is written in a hard style, the author having adopted the unrhymed alliterative line most usually of four accents. The "Vision" occupied Langland from 1362 to 1392, and the various MSS. show many revisings, rewritings, omissions, and additions. Three texts or editions are known which may be affirmed to have proceeded from the author. There are forty-five manuscripts extant. Skeat's edition of the A, the B, and the C texts has been published by the Early English Text Society, and he has issued the three texts together, with a volume of introductions and notes, through the Clarendon Press. A full glossary is given in vol. ii. pp. 569–621.

Lilly, John (circa 1553–1600).—THE DRAMATIC WORKS of John Lilly (The Euphuist). With Notes and Some Account of his Life and Writings. By F. W. Fairholt. 2 vols. 1892.

There are ten plays extant which have been attributed to Lilly, but Mr. Fairholt is of opinion that "A Warning for Faire Women" (1599) bears no trace of Lilly's style and is by an anonymous author. He also thinks "The Maid's Metamorphosis" (1600) "is evidently the production of another mind," and neither of them has been included in this edition of Lilly's dramas. The eight here reprinted are—

	Vol.	Page
1. CAMPASPE	I.	87
The subject of the play is taken from Pliny's "Natural History," lib. xxxv. c. 36 (vol. vi. p. 259).

| 2. ENDIMION . . . . | I. | 1 |
This has a second title, "The Man in the Moone," a phrase used to signify "any wild story, out of the ordinary rules of criticism."

| 3. GALLATHEA . . . . | I. | 215 |
| 4. LOVE'S METAMORPHOSIS . . . . | II. | 213 |
Collier ("History of Dramatic Poetry," vol. iii. p. 189) inclines to think that this "was probably the work of Lyly at an advanced "period of life, and that it had not the recommendation of the or- "dinary, though affected, graces of his style."

| 5. MOTHER BOMBIE . . . . | II. | 70 |

			Vol.	Page
6. MYDAS	. . . .		II.	1

This produces many of Lilly's characteristic " wonderful beliefs" as to animals. In act i. scene ii. (vol. ii. p. 14), he writes: " Hares "we cannot be, because they are male one yeare, and the next "female, wee change not our sex."

7. SAPHO AND PHAO	. . . .	I.	153
8. WOMAN IN THE MOONE, THE	. . . .	II.	149

This, according to the Prologue, was the first work of the author:

" The first he had in Phœbus' holy bowre,
" But not the last, unlesse the first displease."

It is argued that " the idea of this whole play being considered as its author's " dream probably gave Shakespeare the notion for his ' Midsummer-Night's Dream.' " Lilly says in the Prologue, " Remember, all is but a Poet's dreame."

Lilly's (or Lyly's) success as a dramatist was considerable. John Blount, who edited six of his comedies, styles him " the only rare poet of the time, the witty, " comical, facetious, quick, and unparalleled John Lilly."

Ben Jonson, in his verses on Shakespeare, treats Lilly as taking precedence of Kyd or Marlowe:

" If I thought my judgment were of yeares,
" I should commit thee surely with thy peers,
" And tell how far thou didst our Lyly outshine,
" Or sporting Kyd, or Marlowe's mighty line."

Malone, Bishop Percy, Hazlitt, Lamb, and Longfellow all praised him.

Lobeira, Vasco de (*ob.* 1403?).—AMADIS OF GAUL. Translated from the Spanish Version of Garciordonez de Montalvo. By Robert Southey. A New Edition. 3 vols. 1872.

Hallam states that Lobeira's death is generally fixed in 1325, although it else-where seems that Lobeira received knighthood from King John I. of Portugal in 1386; but be this as it may, " a new era of romance began with the ' Amadis.' " " This famous romance," says Hallam in his Literature of Europe, " was in its day " almost as popular as the Orlando Furioso, and was translated piecemeal into French "between 1540 and 1557 and into English in 1619." He adds: " The four books " by Vasco de Lobeyra grew to twenty by successive additions which have been held " by lovers of the romance far inferior to the original, and which deserve at least " the blame, or praise, of making the entire work unreadable by the most patient or " the most idle of mankind."

In this edition the translator ends (in the fourth book) with the celebration of the marriage of Amadis and Oriana, " and leaves the reader to infer that they, like the " heroes of every nursery tale, lived very happy after."

As to the remainder, Southey styles the additions " one romance growing out of " another as clumsily as a young oyster upon the back of its parent."

" Amadis of Gaul" was one of the three romances spared by the curate from the

condemnation to fire which overtook the bulk of the pernicious literature which had turned the brains of the unhappy Don Quixote. This was spared because it was the first of its kind and the best. Amadis is the central figure of Spanish and Portuguese romance, as Arthur is of British or Charlemagne of French romance.

Southey has reduced the original to about half its length in the original folio "by "abridging the words, not the story; by curtailing the dialogue, avoiding all reca- "pitulations of the past action, consolidating many of those single blows which have "no reference to armorial anatomy, and passing over the occasional moralizings of "the author."

Lovelace, Richard (1618–1658).—LUCASTA. The poems of Richard Lovelace, Esq. [With Portrait.] Now first Edited, and the Text carefully Revised. With some Account of the Author, and a few Notes. By W. Carew Hazlitt. 1864.

The poet fought for the king (Charles I.), but in 1648 was imprisoned for political reasons for a year, and ten years later died in great poverty in Gunpowder Alley, near Shoe Lane, in London.

The biographical memoir is given pp. xi.–xxxvii.

Lucasta, to whom a large number of the poems relate or were addressed, was probably the same lady as the poet's Amarantha. It is surmised that the gentlewoman's name was Lucy Sacheverell, whom Lovelace called his Lux Casta. She was a person of great beauty and fortune. Alexis in the "Amarantha" (pp. 60–74) is the poet himself.

It is curious to notice that in the first edition of "Lucasta," published in 1649, Amarantha is misprinted Aramantha on the title-page. (See *fac-simile* in this edition immediately after the "Contents.")

The two best reputed of his poems are "To Althea. From Prison" (p. 117) and "To Lucasta. Going to the Warres" (p. 26).

H. Morley describes him as the pattern of a brilliant cavalier poet, and adds that when only of two years' standing and eighteen years old, the king, visiting Oxford, is said to have made him M.A. for his beauty at the request of a great lady.

Malory, Sir Thomas (1430– ?).—LA MORT D'ARTHURE. The History of King Arthur and of the Knights of the Round Table. Compiled by Sir Thomas Malory, Knt. Edited from the Text of the Edition of 1634, with Introduction and Notes. By Thomas Wright. Third Edition. 3 vols. 1889.

Sir Thomas Malory, who was probably born about 1430, compiled these romances "early in 1470, or more than fifteen years" before Caxton printed them in 1485. For a full account of Caxton's edition, of which "only one complete copy is "known," and of Wynkyn de Worde's edition of 1498, see Dibdin's "Typographical "Antiquities" (vol. i. pp. 241–255), and the same author's "Bibliotheca Spenceri- "ana" (vol. iv. pp. 403–409). Dibdin includes several interesting wood-cuts in his description of the latter edition.

The edition under description is printed from a reprint in 1634, when "the last

"of the black-letter editions was published in three parts, in 4to, with three separate "titles." It has been also "collated with the text of Caxton," and any important variations are shown in the notes.

"The Prologue" (vol. i. pp. xxvii.–xxxi.) and "the Preface of William Caxton to "the Christian Reader" (vol. i. pp. xxxii.–xxxiv.) are taken from Caxton's edition, "and are here printed verbatim."

The "Colophon" to Caxton's edition is reprinted, vol. iii. p. 354.

The Morte d'Arthur has been reprinted ten or eleven times. The next to Caxton's edition of 1485 was that of Wynkyn de Worde in 1498, in folio, of which the only known copy is in the Althorp collection, now the property of the city of Manchester, England. The third issue was also by Wynkyn de Worde in 1529, of which the only known copy is in the British Museum.

Of later reprints, the best known are Southey's edition of 1817 and Mr. Thomas Wright's two editions of 1856 and 1866 included in the "Library of Old Authors."

However useful this may be as a popular edition accessible to general readers, all students will rejoice in that triumph of patient and skilful editorship—the four-volume edition brought out by Dr. Oskar Sommer, and published in 1889–91. A copy has recently been added to the Free Library of Philadelphia. Its text is reprinted page for page and line for line from Lord Spencer's copy of Caxton's edition, acquired in 1816 for £325, and now in the Althorp Collection. That copy, unfortunately, has eleven leaves in facsimile. The only complete copy of this first edition is in the library of Mrs. Abbey E. Pope, of Brooklyn, for which she paid £1950. The Trustees of the British Museum bid up to £1800 only, and so let it escape them.

The source of each portion of the cycle of romances is traced by Dr. Sommer with great care and skill.

Marston, John (1575(?)–1634).—THE WORKS of John Marston, Reprinted from the Original Editions. With Notes and Some Account of his Life and Writings. By J. O. Halliwell. 3 vols. 1856.

Little is really known of Marston. His manners were not commendable if the anecdote in Collier's "Annals of the Stage" (vol. i. p. 335) is true. Once, in 1602, when dancing with a lady of Spanish birth, he praised her wit and beauty. When he had done, she "thought to pay him home," and told him she thought he was a poet. "'Tis true," said he, "for poets feigne and lye, and soe do I, when I commended your beauty, for you are exceeding foule."

His dramas are enumerated below:

	Vol.	Page
ANTONIO AND MELLIDA (Part I)	I.	1

> This was published at London in 1602. Marston was satirized
> by Ben Jonson in the "Poetaster" under the name of Crispinus. The
> chief point of attack was the bluster of this and one or two others of
> his plays, which led to anomalies of language. Marston took the casti-
> gation to heart, and the terms that Jonson so ridiculed were not exhib-
> ited in his later plays and works. Jonson and Marston had more than
> one quarrel, but equally had more than one sincere reconciliation.

	Vol.	Page
ANTONIO'S REVENGE	I.	69

This is "The Second Part of the Historie of Antonio and Mel-"lida." A. H. Bullen says of this and "Antonio and Mellida" that "the writing is uneven; detached scenes are memorable, but "there is an intolerable quantity of fustian."

CHESTER'S LOVES MARTYR. (*See* Verses.)

	Vol.	Page
CITY PAGEANT on the Occasion of the Visit Paid by the King of Denmark to James I. in 1606	III.	323

This consists mainly of Latin verses. It is to be found in manuscript in the British Museum.

	Vol.	Page
DUTCH COURTEZAN, THE	II.	107

This was published in 1605. It was originally produced by the "Children of Her Maiesties Revels at Blacke Friars." It was revived by Betterton in 1680 under the title of "The Revenge; or, "A Match in Newgate." Some of the incidents of the story are to be found in the last novel in Painter's "Palace of Pleasure."

	Vol.	Page
EASTWARD HOE. As it was playd in the Black-friers by the Children of Her Maiesties Revels	III.	1

This was "made by Geo. Chapman, Ben. Ionson, Ioh. Marston." This was the play that caused Chapman and Marston to be imprisoned with a threat of having their noses slit and ears cut off for reflections on the Scots which much offended King James I. Ben Jonson voluntarily joined them in their prison, but all three were released without the direful consequences with which they were threatened.

In the third note at the end of vol. iii. is given the passage which caused so much trouble. Commenting on the Scots, the playwrights expressed too openly that they would a hundred thousand of them were in Virginia, as they would find "ten times more comfort of "them there" than in England. This passage, act iii. scene 2 (sometimes entitled scene 3), was speedily cancelled. Jesse, in his "Court of England under the Stuarts" (ed. 1855, i. 52–53), remarks on this passage that "Englishmen were disgusted at the favours lav-"ished by James on the needy Scots, who swarmed southwards "'with pride and hungry hopes completely arm'd.'"

Probably the sentence later (p. 64, l. 15), "'I ken the man weel; "hees one of my thirty pound knights," which was a sneer at those who purchased the honour of knighthood from King James, and the fact that "as the actor spoke these words he mimick'd James's Scotch "accent" equally gave offence.

ENTERTAINMENT. (*See* Lorde and Ladye Huntingdon.)

FAWNE, THE. (*See* Parasitaster.)

Vol. Page

INSATIATE COUNTESSE, THE . . . . III. 103

This was first published in 1613, although some writers have mentioned the date of publication as 1603. The play is not included in
Marston's collected plays published in 1633. The plot and under-
plot are taken from the fourth and fifteenth "Tales" of Bandello,
and both tales are given in Painter's "Palace of Pleasure," Tome ii.
Novels 24 and 26.

LORDE, THE, AND LADYE HUNTINGDON'S ENTERTAINEMENT of their
Right Noble Mother, Alice, Countesse Dowager of Darby, the
firste Nighte of her Honor's Arrivall at the House of Ashby . III. 311

MALCONTENT, THE . . . . II. 193

This was written by John Webster and is included in his "Dra-
"matic Works." It was augmented by Marston, and published in
1604, with "the Additions played by the Kings Maiesties Ser-
"vants." It is supposed that the additions by Marston were made
three or four years before. This play was dedicated to Ben Jonson,
one of the reconciliations between Marston and Jonson having taken
place in 1604, the year in which two editions of this play were
issued. (See p. 39.)

METAMORPHOSIS OF PIGMALIONS IMAGE AND CERTAINE SATYRES, THE . III. 199

The initials "W. K." to the "Dedicatory Verses" stand for W.
Kinsayder, a pseudonym assumed by Marston. The poems are dedicated "To the Worlds Mightie Monarch, Good Opinion." These
pieces were originally published in 1598.
The satires are five in number.

PARASITASTER; or, The Fawne . . . . II. 1

This is partly founded on Boccaccio's "Tales," Day iii. Nov. 3.

PIGMALION. (See Metamorphosis.)

ROSALINS COMPLAINT. (See Verses.)

SATIRES. (See Metamorphosis, and Scourge of Villanie.)

SCOURGE, THE, OF VILLANIE. Three Bookes of Satyres . . . III. 239

The dedication is unusual: "To his most esteemed and best be-
"loved Selfe. Dat Dedicatque." It is pretended (see satire vi.)
to be written to throw discredit on amatory verses. Whether that
was so or not, the Archbishop of Canterbury in 1599 ordered this
work and Marston's "Pigmalion" to be burnt. The "Order for
"Conflagration" is quoted in Notes and Queries, series iii. vol. xii.
p. 436.

SOPHONISBA. (See Wonder of Women.)

VERSES FROM CHESTER'S LOVES MARTYR; or, Rosalins Complaint,
published in the year 1601 . . . . III. 327

Vol. Page

WHAT YOU WILL . . . . I. 217
This was published in 1607, and is printed in vol. ii. of Dilke's
"Collection of Old Plays."
Langbaine remarks that "Francisco's zanying the person and hu-
"mour of Albano is an incident in several plays, as Mr. Cowley's
"'Guardian,' 'Albumazer,' etc., tho' I presume" (he adds) "the de-
"sign was first copy'd from Plautus his Amphitruo; this I take to
"be one of our author's best plays."

WONDER, THE, OF WOMEN; OR, THE TRAGEDIE OF SOPHONISBA . . I. 145
This is a "blood-curdling tragedy," founded on the historical accounts of Livy and Cornelius Nepos; also set forth in Sir Walter
Raleigh's "History of the World." Sophonisba, a Carthaginian
lady and wife of the king of Numidia, was taken prisoner in 203 B.C.
by Massinissa, her former lover. For political reasons Massinissa
gave her poison, from the effects of which she died.

Mather, Cotton (1663–1728).—THE WONDERS OF THE INVISIBLE
WORLD. Being an Account of the Tryals of Several Witches
lately Executed in New-England. (pp. 1–198.)

With this work is bound a copy of Increase Mather's "A Further Account of the
"Tryals of the New-England Witches." (*See* below.)

The scene of the popular delusion described in these works is Massachusetts, and
recounts the anti-witch doings of Salem and Andover. In Salem alone nineteen
persons were executed for witchcraft, as were also two dogs, and one other person
was "pressed" to death for refusing to plead.

The author never repented of the part he had taken in these proceedings, but
reaffirmed his credulity in two books published long subsequently to the discovery of
the fraudulent means by which the delusion had been bolstered up.

This voluminous writer is said to have published three hundred and eighty-two
pieces (sermons, essays, and volumes) in his lifetime. His "Invisible World" and
his "Magnalia, or Ecclesiastical History of New England," were among the most
important of his writings. He was an enthusiast on very ordinary subjects, so his
persistency and apparently sincere belief on the topic of witchcraft is intelligible if
deplorable. The frenzy lasted about fifteen months, and only materially abated
when charges of witchcraft were brought against members of the Mather family and
relations of the governor. At one time two hundred and fifty persons were in prison
on this charge.

Mather, Increase (1635–1723).—A FURTHER ACCOUNT OF THE
TRYALS OF THE NEW-ENGLAND WITCHES. With the Observations of a Person who was upon the Place several Days when
the suspected Witches were first taken into Examination. (pp.
199–217.) To which is added, Cases of Conscience Concerning Witchcrafts and Evil Spirits Personating Men. Written at
the Request of the Ministers of New-England. (pp. 219–291.)

This was originally published in 1693. When the labours of Dr. Cotton Mather were becoming discredited, the aid of Dr. Cotton's father, Dr. Increase Mather, was called into requisition. This author and his son persisted obstinately in the opinions they had published, and "looked upon the reactionary feeling as a triumph of Satan " and his kingdom."

Mather, Increase.—REMARKABLE PROVIDENCES illustrative of the earlier days of American Colonisation. With Introductory Preface by George Offor. 1890.

Increase Mather was one of the number who refused to conform after the Restoration, and came to America, where he was chosen minister of the New Church at Boston. He was president of Harvard College from 1684 to 1701. He was father of Cotton Mather, whose well-remembered motto over a library door was " Be short." Of his work on " Remarkable Providences," we find that performances still attributed to spirit-rapping, trances, second-sight, and so on were all well known to the spiritual pioneers in New England. The *North American Review* in 1857 reviewed this book, and regarded it as a " capital contribution to spiritualistic literature in its col- " lection of test cases, its accurate collection of marvels, and its delightful credulity." It gives a faithful portrait of the state of society when the belief in a peculiar providence and personal intercourse between this world and that which is unseen was more fully believed in than to-day.

Musæus.—DIVINE POEM. *See* Chapman.

Newcastle, Margaret, Duchess of (*ob.* 1673).—THE LIVES OF WILLIAM CAVENDISHE, DUKE OF NEWCASTLE, AND OF HIS WIFE, MARGARET, DUCHESS OF NEWCASTLE. [With Portrait.] Written by the Thrice Noble and Illustrious Princess, Margaret, Duchess of Newcastle. Edited with a Preface and Occasional Notes by Mark Antony Lower. 1872.

The full title to the Life of the duke, as printed in 1667, employed one hundred and fifty-nine words. That of the Life of the duchess employed one hundred and twenty-one words.

Opinions as to the value of these Lives have varied. The University of Cambridge in acknowledging a presentation copy lauded it to the skies. Pepys styles it the " ridiculous history of my Lord Newcastle, wrote by his wife : which shows her to be " a mad, conceited, ridiculous woman, and he an asse to suffer her to write what she " writes to him and of him." Charles Lamb held the book to be " both good and " rare—no casket being rich enough, no casing sufficiently durable, to honour and " keep safe such a jewel."

The Life of the duchess forms " the eleventh and last book" of a volume " Written " by the thrice Noble, Illustrious, and Excellent Princess, The Lady Marchioness of " Newcastle," entitled " Natures Pictures drawn by Fancies Pencil to the Life," in which volume it is stated " there are several feigned stories of Natural Descrip- " tions, as Comical, Tragical, and Tragi-comical, Poetical, Romancical, Philosophical,

"and Historical, both in Prose and Verse, some all Verse, some all Prose, some
"mixt, partly Prose and partly Verse. Also, there are some Morals and some Dia-
"logues; but they are as the advantage Loaves of Bread as a Baker's Dozen; and
"a true Story at the latter End, wherein there is no feinins." This true story is
the Life of the duchess. The duke is best known by his "System of Horseman-
"ship." He and his duchess regarded each other with extravagant admiration, and
whether with her bevy of maids of honour, ready at all hours to register her grace's
"conceptions," she was "a mad duchess," or, as Walpole styles her, "a fertile pedant
"with an unbounded passion for scribbling," or, as Lamb deemed her, "a princely
"woman, the thrice noble Margaret of Newcastle, never to be mentioned without
"praise," must be left for each to decide for himself.

A recent reviewer said "she wrote various works, among which are poems and
"plays remarkable for absurdity and bad grammar."

The authoress, according to Mr. Walpole, seldom revised the copies of her works,
"lest it should disturb her following conceptions."

Of her, as a woman, he testifies "her grace's literary labours have drawn down less
"applause than her domestic virtues."

Overbury, Sir Thomas (1581–1613).—The Miscellaneous Works, in Prose and Verse, of Sir Thomas Overbury, Knt. Now First Collected. Edited, with Notes, and a Biographical Account of the Author, by Dr. Edward F. Rimbault. 1890.

The life of this unfortunate poet and "friend" is of greater interest to the general
reader than the works he left behind. His friendship with Carr, the favourite of
James I. and afterwards Earl of Somerset, and his unsuccessful efforts to prevent that
nobleman from marrying the Countess of Essex, are a melancholy story. The author
was poisoned in the Tower, and the earl and countess were convicted of the crime
but pardoned. For some reason not satisfactorily ascertained, his murder was so
wrapped up in mystery, that Somerset and his wife, the king, and all are to this day
heavily weighted with the charge of having been guilty of this crime. Only some
inferior agents in the affair, like the poisoner, Mrs. Turner, were executed.

The works comprised in this edition are:

Page
1. CHARACTERS 47
    Hallam considers "A faire and happy Milk-mayd" (p. 118) the best of
    the characters.

2. CRUMMS FAL'N FROM KING JAMES'S TABLE. Or, His Table Talk, princi-
    pally Relating to Religion, Embassyes, State-Policy, &c. . . . 253
    The original is in Sir Thomas Overbury's own handwriting.

3. ELEGIES 5

4. NEWES FROM ANY WHENCE; or, Old Truth, Under a Supposall of Noveltie . 171

5. REMEDY OF LOVE, The First and Second Part of The 201
    This is a paraphrase of the first and second parts of Ovid's "Remedy of
    "Love."

Page
6. THE XVII. PROVINCES AS THEY STOOD ANNO DOM., 1609. The Treatie
of Peace being then on foote 221

7. WIFE; with Addition of many new Elegies upon his [the Author's] vntimely
and much lamented death. As Also New Newes, and diuers more
Characters (never before annexed) written by himselfe and other much
learned Gentlemen. 1616 33

This was written to dissuade Somerset from marrying the Countess of
Essex. One of the last lines—

" He comes too neere, that comes to be denide,"—

hinted too broadly the charges made against Overbury of having failed in a
desired intrigue with the Countess of Rutland. The line became almost a
proverb.

Quarles, Francis (1592–1644).—ENCHIRIDION : Containing Institutions

DIVINE { CONTEMPLATIVE.
PRACTICAL.

MORAL { ETHICAL.
ŒCONOMICAL.
POLITICAL.

Written by Francis Quarles. 1856.

This is a " handbook" of aphorisms on religious and ethical topics, described in the
Retrospective Review (vol. v. p. 182) as "perhaps the best collection of maxims in
" the English language." It is in four books, each containing one hundred aphorisms. In the first edition, published in 1640, there were three books only, and the
volume was dedicated to Elizabeth, the daughter of Archbishop Ussher, or Usher.
In 1641 a second edition was published with four " centuries of essays," and the
volume was dedicated to Prince Charles, afterwards King Charles II. The dedication to the prince is given before book i. (pp. 1–2), and that to Mrs. Elizabeth
Usher was remitted to the beginning of book ii., and is given in this edition, pp.
47–48. It is stated that the " Enchiridion" rivalled Quarles's " Emblems" in popularity. H. D. Thoreau in his Letters (1865) praises the Enchiridion very highly.

Sackville, Thomas, Earl of Dorset (1536–1608).—THE WORKS of Thomas Sackville, Lord Buckhurst, afterwards Lord Treasurer to Queen Elizabeth and Earl of Dorset. Edited by the Hon. and Rev. Reginald W. Sackville-West. 1859.

Politics formed the main interest and work of Sackville's life. He it was who
was selected by Queen Elizabeth to announce to Mary, Queen of Scots, that she
would be executed. .

His connection with literature is interesting. He wrote the first English tragedy
in blank verse. It could hardly be hoped it would live long. In act i. scene ii.,

for example, there are eight speeches only and a " chorus" of twenty-four lines at the end, but those eight speeches are composed respectively of thirty-two, thirteen, thirty-one, seventy-one, ninety-nine, ninety, thirty-one, and two, lines respectively, making a goodly total of three hundred and ninety-three lines, divided into nine speeches. It was entitled " Ferrex and Porrex," but had been surreptitiously printed under the title of " Gorboduc." It was acted in 1561, and printed (very incorrectly) as " Gorboduc" in 1563, but reprinted in a correct edition in 1571. The play concludes with a remark by Eubulus, the secretary to the king, compressed within exactly one hundred lines.

A more important literary work was his planning the celebrated " Myrrovre for " Magistrates." He wrote a poetical preface called an " Induction" (pp. 93–123). The work was to show by examples " with how greuous plagues, Vices are punished " in great Princes and Magistrates, and how frayle and unstable worldly prosperitie " is found where Fortune seemeth most highly to favour." Sackville, however, contributed nothing but the Induction and one of the " Legends," and had to leave the execution of the work to Richard Baldwin and George Ferrers. The Induction was transferred to the middle of the second volume and changed to suit its altered position. The Legend in the " Mirror for Magistrates" is called " The Complaynt " of Henry, Duke of Buckingham" (pp. 124–161 in this vol.). This duke was the chief supporter of Richard III., but he afterwards conspired against the king, and was beheaded in the year 1484.

Sandys, George (1577–1643).—THE POETICAL WORKS. [With Portrait.] Now first Collected. With Introduction and Notes by the Rev. Richard Hooper. 2 vols. 1872.

The works included in these volumes (which have a continuous pagination) are :

	Page
A PARAPHRASE UPON JOB	1
THE PSALMS OF DAVID	79
ECCLESIASTES	311
THE SONG OF SOLOMON	335
THE LAMENTATIONS OF JEREMIAH	357
THE SONGS COLLECTED OUT OF THE OLD AND NEW TESTAMENTS	373
A POEM: DEO OPT. MAX.	403
CHRIST'S PASSION: A TRAGEDY	407
TWO SHORT PIECES IN THE APPENDIX	505

The translations, especially of Job, have been very highly esteemed; and Dr. Burney wrote of the Paraphrase of the Psalms, " The Psalms " are put into better verse than they ever appeared in before or since." They are one of the books which King Charles I. delighted to read whilst he was a prisoner in Carisbrooke Castle. At the end of volume i. are given " New Tunes and a Thorough Bass," by Henry Lawes, the celebrated musician, for use to the Psalms as paraphrased by Sandys.

The subject of the tragedy of " Christ's Passion" was first employed in a

drama in Greek by Apollinarius of Laodicea, bishop of Hierapolis, and after him by St. Gregory Nazianzen (329-390), though the authorship is disputed in the latter case, and scholars declare "that the Χριστὸς πάσχων " usually included in his works is certainly not genuine." The tragedy here given is a translation of "Christus Patiens," one of the three dramas in Latin written by Hugo Grotius (1583-1645), of whom Sandys wrote, " but Hugo Grotius of late hath transcended all, on this argument : whose " steps afar off I follow."

The poetry of George Sandys is eulogized by Dryden, Pope, Warton, and other writers. He travelled a great deal in Constantinople, Greece, Egypt, Holy Land, and Italy in his younger days.

Selden, John (1584-1654).—THE TABLE-TALK of John Selden. With a Biographical Preface and Notes by S. W. Singer, F.S.A. To which is added Spare Minutes, or Resolved Meditations and Premeditated Resolutions. By Arthur Warwick. 1890.

This work was compiled by Richard Milward, a secretary or amanuensis of Selden, and contains reports of Selden's utterances during the last twenty years of his life. Dr. Johnson considered Selden's " Table Talk" better than any of the French Ana. Selden possessed one execrable habit which all owners of books would reprobate, for it is recorded that when his library was presented to Oxford, and arrived at the Bodleian, on opening some of the volumes several pairs of spectacles were found which Selden must have put in as book-marks and forgotten where he had placed them.

This volume was described in the title-page of the original edition (1689) as "Table-Talk: being the Discourses of John Selden, Esq. Being His Sense of " various Matters of Weight and high Consequence; relating especially to Religion "and State." The manuscript must have been prepared for publication soon after Selden's death, but was not printed until 1689, nine years after the death of the compiler.

There are one hundred and fifty-five heads or titles in the table of contents (pp. lxxxix.-xciii.).

Some of his ideas are quaint, as the instruction, " In quoting of Books, quote such " Authors as are usually read ; others you may read for your own Satisfaction, but not "name them." He preached differently from his practice, for many of the books he freely quoted from were most recondite. His opinion on marriage will bear enforcement nowadays: " Of all Actions of a Man's Life, his Marriage does least con- "cern other people, yet of all Actions of our Life 'tis most meddled with by other " People."

SPARE MINUTES. By Rev. Arthur Warwick . . . p. 171

The author was a clergyman, and the style of the work is singular. It is reviewed in the *Retrospective Review*, vol ii. p. 45.

Southwell, Robert (1561?-1595).—THE POETICAL WORKS, now first completely edited by William B. Turnbull, Esq., of Lincoln's Inn, Barrister-at-Law. 1856.

The life of this Jesuit priest and poet is probably of considerably more interest than his poems. These are the subject of an article in the *Retrospective Review*, vol. iv. p. 267. After he had been received into the Society of Jesus and ordained priest, he returned to England in order to administer the Sacraments to the Catholics. This was a dangerous duty, as by an Act of Elizabeth any subject of the queen who had been ordained a Roman Catholic priest since the first year of her accession, and resided in England more than forty days, was guilty of treason, and incurred the penalty of death. He was betrayed by one Anne Bellamy, the daughter of one of the Catholics at whose house Southwell celebrated Mass and gave instructions. Her conduct with Richard Topcliffe, the chief officer engaged in enforcing the penal laws against Catholics, has been regarded as ending in the abandonment both of her faith and her virtue. Anyhow, Topcliffe received information of Southwell's visits to the Bellamys, and tracked him and led him back to London. He was cruelly used in prison, and after some three years he was hanged at Tyburn.

His principal poem is " Saint Peter's Complaint," which was published with " Mary " Magdalen's Tears and other works of the Author R. S." in 1634. Among earlier critics, Hall in his Satires was almost alone in ridiculing the author's poems, and by " modern critics Southwell's poetry has been rarely underrated. James Russell " Lowell stands almost alone in pronouncing ' St. Peter's Complaint' to be a drawl of " thirty pages of maudlin repentance."

Spence, Joseph (1699-1768).—ANECDOTES, OBSERVATIONS, AND CHARACTERS OF BOOKS AND MEN. [With Portrait.] Collected from the conversation of Mr. Pope, and other eminent Persons of his time. With Notes, and a Life of the Author. By Samuel Weller Singer. Second edition, 1858.

This is a verbatim reprint of Mr. Singer's first edition, published in 1820. A posthumous edition by Malone and one by Singer were issued in 1820, on the same day. Malone's edition was only a selection, and when the verbatim reprint of Singer's 1820 edition appeared in 1858, it was much regretted by the critics that " a carefully " revised, collated, and annotated edition" had not been issued instead.

Spence was author of " Moralities" and also of " Crito; or, A Dialogue on " Beauty," published in 1752 under the pseudonym of " Sir Harry Beaumont." Spence figures as the " Dervise of the Groves" in the Rev. James Ridley's " Tales " of the Genii" under the not inscrutable anagram of Phesoj Enceps. Mr. Ridley gives an accurate and interesting delineation of the character and country retreat of Spence. He was in request as a travelling companion or tutor with such men as Charles Sackville, earl of Middlesex, afterwards second duke of Dorset, the second duke of Newcastle, and other young noblemen. His home amusement was gardening. He succeeded Warton in the chair of poetry at Oxford, a position he occupied for two periods of five years each. " Without his Notes much of the literary history of the

"eighteenth century, and especially that of Pope, his immediate circle, and his an-
"tagonists, would have been irretrievably lost." The book presents "an admirable
"view of the dominant literary and critical tendencies of the eighteenth century."

Before the original manuscript was published, a copy was communicated to Dr.
Johnson, who used many particulars in his Lives of Pope and Addison. It was
subsequently transcribed for Malone, who used it in preparing his Life of Dryden.
It was only after an expiration of fifty-two years from Spence's death that this
important contribution to literary history was printed in full. (*See* Dictionary of
National Biography.)

Suckling, Sir John (1608–1643).—THE POEMS, PLAYS, AND OTHER
REMAINS of Sir John Suckling. [With Portrait.] With a
Copious Account of the Author, Notes, and an Appendix of
Illustrative Pieces. 2 vols. 1892.

Suckling, among other virtues, possessed a great admiration for Shakespeare, imitated him, praised, and quoted him in all the polished circles of the day, of which
he was a distinguished ornament. He was reckless and extravagant to an extreme
and addicted to gambling, to pursue which he would lie in bed all day with a pack
of cards to obtain by practice the most perfect knowledge and management of their
powers. He commented severely on his own folly in his poem, "A Session of the
"Poets :"

> "Suckling next was called, but did not appear,
> "But straight one whispered Apollo i' th' ear,
> "That of all men living he cared not for 't,
> "He loved not the Muses so well as his sport.
> "And prized black eyes, or a lucky hit
> "At bowls, above all the trophies of wit."

The works included in this edition are enumerated below in alphabetical order:

		Vol.	Page
1. AGLAURA		I.	85

This tragi-comedy has two or three happenings to be remembered by. It was printed in folio, with wide margins, and this being
a novelty, was ridiculed in the "Musarum Deliciæ," and compared
to a baby lodged in the great bed of Ware, or to a small picture in a
large frame. It is also said to have been the first play acted in England with scenes, scenes having been theretofore confined to Masques.
Again, it has two fifth acts, and by using one or the other, the play
is a tragedy or a comedy.

| 2. APPENDIX | | II. | 253 |
| 3. BRENNORALT | | II. | 73 |

This was first published under the title of the "Discontented Colo-
"nel." The author is indebted to Shakespeare and Balzac's
"Letters" for entire lines "borrowed" without acknowledgment.

Vol.   Page

4. COPPY, A, OF A LETTER FOVND IN THE PRIVY LODGEINGS AT
    WHITEHALL. London. 1641 . . . . II.   225

This was written to Mr. German in 1640. It was translated into
French, and included in an edition of the "Eikon Basilike" in
1649.

5. ELEGIE, AN, VPON THE DEATH OF THE RENOWNED SIR IOHN
    SVTLIN. 1642 . . . . II.   279

6. FOUR FUGITIVES MEETING; or, The Discourse amongst my Lord
    Finch, Sir Francis Windebank, Sir Iohn Sucklin, and Doctor
    Roane, as they accidentally met in France, with a detection of
    their severall pranks in England. 1641 . . . . . II.   265

7. GOBLINS, THE . . . . II.   1

This was never completed, and gives small promise of a successful play. The idea of the play seems to be borrowed from Shakespeare. The lines that most attract attention are in act. iii. (p. 29):

      "The Prince of Darkness is a gentleman,
      "Mahu, Mahu is his name,"

a direct quotation, apparently, from King Lear, act iii. scene iv. line
135. On this, refer to Dr. Furness's Variorum "King Lear," p. 198.

8. LETTER, A, Sent by Sir Iohn Svckling from France, Deploring his
    sad Estate and flight. With a discoverie of the plot and con-
    spiracie, intended By him and his adherents against England.
    1641.

This was a lampoon supposed to have been written by one William
Norris (*Notes and Queries*, series ii. vol. xi. p. 204), in which are
recited many events of the poet's life. Sir John Suckling had rendered himself particularly obnoxious to the Parliamentarians.

9. LETTERS . . . . II.   171

10. NEWES FROM SIR JOHN SVCKLIN, Being a Relation of His Conver-
    sion from a Papist to a Protestant. Also, What Torments he
    endured by those of the Inquisition in Spaine, And how the
    Lord Lekeux, his Accuser, was strucken dumbe, hee going to
    have the Sentence of Death passe upon him. Sent in a Letter
    to the Lord Conway, now being in Ireland. 1641 . . . II.   275

This is altogether a fictitious performance "of the Puritans."

11. POEMS . . . . I.   1

"A Session of the Poets" (p. 6) is perhaps Suckling's best known
piece, and has been since imitated by numberless writers. It was
an original idea at the time when it was written. Many consider his
ballad, "Upon a Wedding" (p. 34) his masterpiece. "Tell Me, Ye
"Juster Deities" (p. 75), and "When, Dearest, I but Think of Thee"
(p. 74), are highly regarded.

	Vol.	Page
12. RELIGION, AN ACCOUNT OF	II.	235

This is an unpleasant sort of letter, described by Suckling himself as one "which frighted the lady into a cold sweat, and which had " like to have made himself an atheist at Court and the Earl of Dor- " set no very good Christian."

| 13. SAD ONE, THE . . . . | II. | 135 |

This is an unfinished tragedy, but few regret its non-completion, as it is incredible that it ever could have held the stage.

| 14. SUCKLINGTON FACTION, THE; or (Svcklings) Roaring Boyes . . | II. | 275 |

This is a broadside (here reproduced) in the centre of which is an engraving representing two cavaliers in the dress and flowing hair so offensive to the Roundheads. The text is in curious contrast to the engraving.

Warwick, Rev. Arthur. (*See* Selden.)

Webster, John.—THE DRAMATIC WORKS. Edited by William Hazlitt. 4 vols. 1857.

Little is known of Webster except that he lived in the sixteenth century, occupied a high rank as a dramatist, and wrote the majority of his pieces in concert with other writers.

The plays, etc., in this edition, including "The Thracian Wonder," and " The "Weakest goeth to the Wall," both of which are omitted in Dyce's edition of Webster, are :

	Vol.	Page
(*a*) APPIUS AND VIRGINIA: A Tragedy	III.	123

The story here dramatized is the fifth novel in Painter's " Palace "of Pleasure." Mr. Hazlitt mentions that Webster's play was "adapted" by Betterton in 1679 under the title of "The Unjust "Judge; or, Appius and Virginia." This story was used by Dennis in 1709, by Henry Crisp in 1754, by John Moncrieff in 1755, by Francis Brooke in 1756, and lastly, and most successfully of all, by Sheridan Knowles in 1820.

| (*b*) CURE, A, FOR A CUCKOLD: A Pleasant Comedy. Written by Webster and William Rowley . . . . | IV. | 1 |

Webster in this play, which was not printed till 1661, and Massinger in his " Parliament of Love," have apparently both borrowed from a common source. They were contemporaries, and it is improbable that either " copied" the play of the other. As both their plays were published posthumously, it cannot be determined which was written first.

<table>
<tr><td></td><td></td><td>Vol.</td><td>Page</td></tr>
</table>

(c) DEUILS LAW-CASE, THE; or, When Women goe to Law, the Deuill is full of Businesse: A new Tragecomœdy . . . . III.   1

This was published in 1623, and was apparently written about the same time.

(d) MALCONTENT, INDUCTION TO THE . . . . IV.   101

"The Malcontent" (*see* p. 28) is treated by John Marston as one of his own plays, and is included in his "Dramatic Works." The title-page describes the play as "augmented by Iohn Marston, with the "additions played by the Kings Maiesties servants, written by Iohn "Webster," and it was published in 1604. Mr. Hazlitt says, "It is "impossible to determine which were Marston's 'augmentations' and "which were Webster's 'additions.'" The "Induction" was entirely Webster's, and that only is here printed.

(e) [MALFI.] THE TRAGEDY OF THE DVTCHESSE OF MALFY. . . . The perfect and exact Coppy, with diuerse things Printed, that the length of the Play would not beare in the Presentment . . II.   145

This celebrated play has suffered many alterations. It was first "violently" altered by Theobald (1733) into a tragedy called "The "Fatal Secret," when he took "as much of Webster's writing as he "could turn to account." It was "reconstructed for the stage" in 1850, and produced by Mr. Phelps and Miss Glyn; and some "years "later was played in Philadelphia with Miss Emma Waller as the "duchess."

(f) MONUMENTS OF HONOR . . . . III.   22

This "City Pageant" was published in 1624, with a descriptive title composed of one hundred and twenty-nine words, of which a reprint is given p. 225. Only one original copy, possessed by the Duke of Devonshire, is known to exist.

(g) MONVMENTAL COLVMNE, A, ERECTED TO THE LIUING MEMORY OF THE EUER-GLORIOUS HENRY, LATE PRINCE OF WALES . . III.   249

This is one of "three Elegies," published in 1613, "on the most "lamented Death of Prince Henrie," written respectively by Cyril Tourneur, John Webster, and Thomas Heywood.

(h) NORTH-VVARD HOE. By Thomas Decker and Iohn Webster . I.   171

Mr. Dyce writes of this play, and also of "Westward Hoe," "they both are full of life and bustle, and exhibit as curious a pic-"ture of the manners and customs of the time as we shall anywhere "find." The title is a cry of the Thames watermen, who thus vociferated their readiness to take passengers city-wards or Westminster-wards.

(i) ODES. . . . . III.   267

Vol. Page

(*j*) THRACIAN WONDER, THE: A Comical History. Written by John
    Webster and William Rowley . . . . IV. 115

Mr. Dyce "pronounces that, assuredly, not one word of this play
"was written by Webster." It is included in this edition because
it has not been "distinctly appropriated to another writer." It was
probably by a William Webster, who was not related to John Webster.

(*k*) WEAKEST, THE, GOETH TO THE VVALL . . . . . . IV. 213

This is "an alleged work of Webster," and as such is included in
this edition.

(*l*) VVEST-VVARD HOE. Written by Tho: Decker and Iohn Webster . I. 63

This was probably first acted in 1604 or early in 1605. The title
is a cry of the Thames watermen (*see* "Northward Hoe" above), but
was also used insultingly as denoting a person likely to go on a trip
to Tyburn tree.

(*m*) WHITE DIVEL, THE; or, The Tragedy of Paulo Giordano Vrsini,
    Duke of Brachiano, With The Life and Death of Vittoria Co-
    rombona, the famous Venetian Curtizan . . . . . II. 1

This play was afterwards printed under the title of "Injured
"Love; or, The Cruel Husband," by Mr. N. Tate. Tate's "New
"Play" was "The White Divel" with a new name, and, presumably,
with a new claimant to the authorship. In a similar way Tate
altered and dubbed himself "author" of "King Lear."

(*n*) WYAT, THE FAMOVS HISTORY OF SIR THOMAS. With the Corona-
    tion of Queen Mary, and the coming in of King Philip. Writ-
    ten by Thomas Dickers [*sic*] And Iohn Webster . . . I. 1

This play was never reprinted until it was included by Mr. Dyce in
his edition of Webster's works, 1830.

Wither, George (1588–1667).—HALLELUJAH OR, BRITAIN'S SECOND
REMEMBRANCER. With an Introduction by Edward Farr. 1887.

The original title-page of this work (published in 1641) is given p. xxi., and is
as follows:

HALELVIAH | or, | Britans Second Re- | membrancer, bringing to |
    Remembrance (in praisefull | and Pœnitentiall Hymns, Spi- |
    rituall Songs, and Morall-Odes) | Meditations, advancing the
    glory | of God, in the practise of Pietie and | Vertue; and
    applyed to easie Tunes, | to be Sung in Families, &c. | Com-
    posed in a three-fold Volume, by | George Wither. | The first,
    contains Hymns Occasionall. | The second, Hymns Tempo-
    rary. | The third, Hymns Personall. | That all Persons accord-

ing to Their De- | grees, and Qualities, may at all times, and | upon all eminent Occasions, be remem- | bred to praise GOD ; and to be | mindfull of their Duties. |

> One woe is past, the second, passing on ; |
> Beware the third, if this, in vain be gone. |

London, | Printed by I. L. for Andrew Hebb, at the Bell, | in Pauls Church-yard. 1641. |

This poet was a very voluminous writer, and published one hundred and twelve books of pieces, lists of which can be gathered from " Allibone," " Lowndes," " The " British Bibliographer," and similar works. His name is variously spelt Wither, Wyther, and Withers. He was an erratic person ; he fought for Charles I., and then fought for Cromwell. He procured for himself various imprisonments, and soon became strictly a " forgotten poet."

Pope describes him in the " Dunciad" (book i. line 296):

> " He [Eusden] sleeps among the dull of ancient days ;
> " Safe where no criticks damn, no duns molest,
> " Where wretched Withers, Ward, and Gildon rest."

In due course of time, however, the whirligig of fame was reversed, and George Ellis, in his " Specimens," Wordsworth, Southey, and Charles Lamb, each more enthusiastically than his predecessor, found much to praise in Wither, and his works were exhumed and bathed in a sun of generous praise.

Wither is said to be the original of " Castruccio" in the " Cruel Brother" by Sir William Davenant.

Part iii. contains hymns suitable to almost every conceivable occasion. There is not only a hymn " For a Widower or a Widow deprived of a loving Yoke-fellow," but also (hymn xxviii.) " For a Widower or a Widow delivered from a trouble-some Yoke-fellow," " Because deliverance from a troublesome yoke-fellow, is a " benefit neither to be despised nor indiscreetly rejoiced in ; this Hymn" (he adds) "teacheth with what moderation, with what tenderness of heart, and with what " desire we should be affected in such cases." In order to ensure a proper musical treatment, we are instructed to " Sing this as the Lamentation."

Wither, George.—HYMNS AND SONGS OF THE CHURCH. With an Introduction by Edward Farr. 1895.

The original title-page, printed in 1623, is given p. xli., and reads :

The | Hymnes and | Songs Of The | Church. | Divided in two Parts. | The first Part comprehends the Ca- | nonicall Hymnes, and such parcels of | Holy Scripture as may properly be | Sung : with some other ancient | Songs and Creeds. | The second Part consists of Spirituall | Songs, appropriated to the severall

Times | and Occasions, observable in the | Church of Eng-
land. | Translated and Composed | by | G. W. | London : |
Printed by the Assignes of George | Wither. 1623. | Cum
Priuelegio Regis Regali. |

The author added a list of suggested Tunes for the Hymns, and Orlando Gibbons
composed twelve tunes specially for these verses. The tunes are given at the end
of the volume.

Having deserted the Royalists, and being taken prisoner by them whilst fighting
against the king, Wither stood a good chance of being hanged, but Sir John Denham (a brother poet), and some of whose lands had fallen into Wither's clutches,
magnanimously desired his majesty not to hang him, because, so long as Wither lived,
Denham would not be accounted the worst poet in England.

Wither is probably best known for his volume of " Emblems," published in 1635.

There are interesting articles on him in the *Retrospective Review*, vol. vii. p. 219,
and vol. ix. p. 130.

INDEX

ADAM BEL, in Child's Ballads . 18
  in Hazlitt's Poetry of England . 18
  in Hazlitt's Poetry of Scotland . 16
Ælian's Various History, Aubrey's
  "Predictions" translated from . 8
Aglaura, by Suckling . . . 36
Allane-a'-Maut, in Hazlitt's Poetry of
  Scotland 16
Alliteration adopted in Vision of
  Piers Ploughman 23
Allusions, in Camden's Remains . 9
Althorp collection, Lord Spencer's
  copy of La Mort d'Arthur in 26
  property of city of Manchester,
  Eng. 26
Amadis of Gaul, by Vasco de Lo-
  beira 24
  central figure of Spanish and
  Portuguese romance . . 25
  compared with Arthur of British
  and Charlemagne of French
  romance 25
Amarantha, in Lovelace's Poems . 25
American Colonisation, Mather's Re-
  markable Providences illustrative
  of 30
Anagram on Mary Queen of Scots
  (Camden) 10
  on name of Joseph Spence . 35
Anagrams in Camden's Remains . 9
Andover, witch trials in, see Mather,
  Cotton 29
Anecdote of John Marston . . 26
Anecdotes, Observations, and Char-
  acters, by Spence. . . . 35

Animals, Lilly's "wonderful beliefs"
  as to 24
Anonymity of Camden, in his Re-
  mains 10
  of Maid's Metamorphosis . . 23
  of Marston, in Metamorphosis of
  Pigmalion's Image . . 28
  of Spence 35
  of Warning for Faire Women . 23
Antiquities, in Camden's Remains . 9
  of Great Britain, in Drayton's
  Poly-Olbion 14
Antonio and Mellida, by Marston . 26
Antonio's Revenge, by Marston . 27
Aphorisms, in Quarles's Enchiridion 32
Apollinarius of Laodicea, Christ's
  Passion first employed in drama
  by 34
Apparel, in Camden's Remains . 9
Apparitions, in Aubrey's Miscellanies 8
Appius and Virginia, by Webster . 38
Archery in Toxophilus, by Ascham . 7
Armonye of Byrdes, in Hazlitt's Po-
  etry of England 18
Armories, in Camden's Remains . 9
Arthur, History of King: Malory's
  La Mort d'Arthure . . . 25
Arthure, The Awntyrs off, in Hazlitt's
  Poetry of Scotland . . . 16
Artillerie, in Camden's Remains . 9
Ascham, Giles, Seven Letters of . 6
Ascham, Roger, ambassador's secre-
  tary to Court of Charles V. . . 6
  correspondents of, list appended
  to his Letters . . . 6

PAGE

Ascham, Roger, criticism of, in Fuller's Worthies . . . 6
glossary of old words used by . 6
identified with Toxophilus . 7
in Germany during years 1550–
52 5
Latin Poems of . . . 6
Letters, in Latin . . . 6
Life of, in his Works . . 5
Oration on the life and death
of, by Grant . . . 6
pieces omitted from his Works . 5
Queen Elizabeth and . . 6
Report and Discourse of affairs
in Germany . . . 5
criticised by Dr. Campbell . 5
Scholemaster, The . . . 6
criticised in Fuller's Worthies 6
secretary to Edward VI. and
Queen Mary . . . 6
secures annual pension of £10 . 7
Toxophilus 7
criticised in Fuller's Worthies . . . 6
in Retrospective Re-
view . . . 7
identified with Ascham . 7
why written . . . 7
tutor to Princess Elizabeth . 6
Works of 5
Aubrey, John, description of . . 7
Miscellanies, by . . . 7
list of 8

Bacon's, Friar, Brazen - heads
Prophesie, in Hazlitt's Poetry of
England 18
Baldwin, Richard, Myrroure for Mag-
istrates completed by Ferrers and . 33
Bale, John, and authorship of Vision
of Piers Ploughman . . . 23
Ballads, Child's English and Scottish 18
in Hazlitt's Early Popular Poetry
of England 18

PAGE

Ballads in Hazlitt's Early Popular
Poetry of Scotland . . . 16
Ballat of Allane-a'-Maut, in Hazlitt's
Poetry of Scotland . . 16
of Matrymonie, in Hazlitt's Po-
etry of Scotland . . . 16
Ballet of the Nine Nobles, in Hazlitt's
Poetry of Scotland . . 16
shewing how a Dumb Wyff, etc.,
in Hazlitt's Poetry of Scot-
land 16
Balzac, J. L. G. de, his Letters
"borrowed" from, in Suckling's
Brennoralt 36
Basyn, Tale of the, in Hazlitt's Poe-
try of England 18
Batayle of Egyngecourte, in Hazlitt's
Poetry of England . . . 18
Batrachomyomachia, translated by
Chapman 12
Battle of Harlaw, in Hazlitt's Poetry
of Scotland 16
of the dunghill: Polemo-Mid-
dinia, in Drummond's Poems 15
Baxter, Richard, Aubrey's Corps
Candles in Wales, part of a letter
to 8
Beaumont, Sir Harry, pseudonym of
Spence 35
Bellamy, Anne, betrays Southwell . 35
her conduct with Richard Top-
cliffe 35
Berdok, King, in Hazlitt's Poetry of
Scotland 16
Betterton, Thomas, adapts Webster's
Appius 38
revives Marston's Dutch Cour-
tezan 27
Bibliographical notes to poems, in
Hazlitt's Poetry of England . 18
Bibliography of Carew, in his Poems 11
Bibliotheca Hearniana, in Hearne's
Remains 21
Birth of Jack Puffe, in Hazlitt's Poe-
try of England . . . 18

Bliss, Philip, Hearne's Remains collected by 21
Blount, John, describes Lilly as a poet 24
Blows Invisible, in Aubrey's Miscellanies 8
Boccaccio's Tales, Marston's Parasitaster partly founded on . . 28
Bodleian Library, Hearne appointed to post in . . · . 21
   MS. of Browne's Brampton Urns in 9
   Musæus's Hero and Leander in . 12
   receives Selden's library . . 34
Boke of Mayd Emlyn, in Hazlitt's Poetry of England . . . 18
Booke in Meeter of Robin Conscience, in Hazlitt's Poetry of England 18
Book-marks, Selden uses spectacles as 34
Boston, Mass., Increase Mather minister of New Church at . . 30
Brampton Urns, by Browne . . 9
Brennoralt, by Suckling . . . 36
Britain, Camden's Remains Concerning 9
Britain's Second Remembrancer, Wither's Hallelujah; or, . . 40
Britannia, by Camden, . . . 9
British Museum, bid for Malory's Morte d'Arthur . . . 26
   MS. of Browne's Brampton Urns in 9
   MS. of Marston's City Pageant in 27
   possesses third issue of Mort d'Arthure, printed by Wynkyn de Worde 26
   unique copy of Drayton's Harmonie in 15
Brooke, Francis, uses story of Webster's Appius 38
Brooke, Ralph, "corrigenda" of, adopted by Camden . - . 10

Browne, Sir Thomas, and his Religio Medici 9
   Brampton Urns, by . . . 9
   MS. of, in Bodleian and British Museum . . 9
   Hydriotaphia : Urn-Burial, by . 9
   views on women and marriage . 9
Brute, Walter, and Creed of Piers Ploughman 22
Buckhurst, Lord, see Sackville, Thomas.
Buckingham, Henry, Duke of, beheaded for conspiracy . . 33
   Complaint of, in Myrroure for Magistrates 33
Bullen, A. H., criticises works of Marston 27
Burial customs discussed in Browne's Hydriotaphia 9
Burial urns found at Walsingham . 9
Burleigh, Lord, Giles Ascham's letters written to 6
Burney, Dr., on Sandys's Psalms of David 33
Byrdes, The Armonye of, in Hazlitt's Poetry of England . . . 18

Caius, Dr., epitaph on, in Camden's Remains 10
Cambridge University, Caius College founded by Dr. Caius . . 10
   praises Lives of Duke and Duchess of Newcastle . . 30
   Roger Ascham at . . . 6
   Sir John Cheke public orator at . 7
Camden Society named after William Camden . . . . - . 10
Camden, William, adopts Brooke's Corrigenda 10
   Britannia, an estimate of his . 9
   Drayton's Poly-olbion likened to 14
   enlargement of Leland's "Itinerary," . . . 10
   his Remains founded on . 10

INDEX

Camden, William, Disraeli in his
"Calamities" deals with . 10
on his own "Remains" . . 10
Remains Concerning Britain . 9
epigrams in . . . 10
Campaspe, by Lilly . . . 23
Campbell, Dr., on Ascham's Report
and Discourse 5
Canterbury, Archbishop of, orders
works of Marston to be burnt 28
seizes Drayton's Harmonie . 15
Carew, Thomas, and Inigo Jones in-
vent the masque . . . 11
Bibliography of, in his Poems . 11
birth and death, dates of, dis-
puted 11
Cœlum Britannicum: a Masque,
by 11
performed at Whitehall . 11
set to music by Henry
Lawes 11
criticised by Suckling . . 11
Extra Poems from Manuscripts . 11
gossip of Hales of Eton about . 11
Jessopp, Dr., on, in Dictionary
of National Biography . . 11
Memoir of, in his Poems . . 11
Paraphrase of Certain Psalms, by 11
Poems 11
Pope's admiration for . . 11
Carisbrooke Castle, Charles I. im-
prisoned in 33
Carpenters' Tools, Debate of, in Haz-
litt's Poetry of England . . 18
Carr, Robert, see Somerset, Earl of.
Cases of Conscience Concerning
Witchcrafts, by Mather . . 29
Catalogue of Hearne's library, in his
Remains 21
Catholics, Act of Elizabeth as to . 35
Cavendish, William, see Newcastle,
Duke of.
Caxton, William, his Mort d'Arthure
in Dibdin's Typographical An-
tiquities 25

Chapman, George, described as "a
"rough nut" . . . 13
Eastward Hoe, by Jonson, Marston, and 27
estimation of his translation of
Homer 13
Glossarial Index to his classical
translations 12
Hesiod's Works and Days, translated by 11
Homer's Batrachomyomachia,
Hymns, and Epigrams,
translated by . . . 11
Iliads, translated by . . 13
Odysseys, translated by . 13
complaint concerning
his translation . . 14
editions described . 13
imprisoned with Marston and
Jonson for writing Eastward
Hoe 27
Juvenal's Fifth Satire, translated
by 11
Musæus's Hero and Leander,
translated by . . . 11, 12
no record of his life . . . 14
said to be the rival poet referred
to in Shakespeare's Sonnets . 14
translations praised by various
writers 13
Characters, by Overbury . . . 31
Characters of Books and Men, by
Spence 35
Charles I., death of, grieves Drummond 15
delighted with Sandys's Psalms
of David 33
Drummond furnishes men to
fight against . . . 15
Lovelace fought for . . . 25
makes Lovelace M.A. . . 25
Wither fought for . . . 41
Charles, Prince, afterwards Charles
II., Quarles's Enchiridion dedicated to 32

PAGE

Charles V., Ascham's Report and Discourse of the state of Germany under 5

Cheke, Sir John, identified with Philologus 7

Chester, Robert, verses by Marston reprinted from his Love's Martyr 28

Childe of Bristowe, in Hazlitt's Poetry of England 18

Christian IV. of Denmark, Marston writes verses on visit of . . 27

Christ's Passion, by Sandys . . 33

Christus Patiens, drama in Latin by Hugh Grotius 34

Chronicles, Hearne's editions of old English 21

Church and State attacked in The Vision and Creed of Piers Ploughman 22

Church, Harmonie of the, by Drayton 15

Hymns and Songs of the, by Wither 41

City pageant on the King of Denmark's visit to James I. . . 27

Civil war in England and Drummond 15

Clym of the Cleugh, in Poetry of Scotland 16

of the Clough, in Poetry of England 19

Cœlum Britannicum, by Carew . 11

Cokwolds Daunce, in Hazlitt's Poetry of England 19

Coleridge, S. T., praises Chapman's translation of Homer . . 13

says Crashaw inspired second part of Christabel . . . 14

Colkelbie Sow, Tale of the, in Hazlitt's Poetry of Scotland . . 16

Collier, J. P., Annals of the Stage, anecdote of Marston in . . 26

on Lilly's Love's Metamorphosis 23

Colyn Blowbol's Testament, in Hazlitt's Poetry of England . . 19

Combat, literary, between Ralph Brooke and Camden . . . 10

PAGE

Commonyng of Ser John Mandevelle, in Hazlitt's Poetry of England 18, 19

Constantinople, Sandys travelled in 34

Converse with Angels, etc., in Aubrey's Miscellanies . . . 8

Cooke, Thomas, translates Hesiod's Georgics 12

Coppy of a Letter found at Whitehall, by Suckling 37

Corps-Candles in Wales, in Aubrey's Miscellanies 8

Correspondents of Roger Ascham's, list of, in his Letters . . . 6

Country life, old English, Herrick noted for descriptions of . . 22

Cowley, Abraham, and Marston's What You Will 29

Crashaw, Richard, Complete Works 14

edition of his poems by Grosart 14

fertile imagination of . . 14

poems drawn on by Milton, Pope, and Coleridge . . 14

Creed of Piers Ploughman, by Langland . . . . . 22 '

Crisp, Henry, uses story of Webster's Appius 38

Criticism, eighteenth century, in Spence's Anecdotes . . 36

in Hearne's Remains . . 21

of Carew, in Suckling's Session of the Poets 11

of Drayton's Poly-Olbion, by Ellis 14

of Hearne, in Gibbon's Posthumous Works 21

of Herrick, in Hallam's Literature of Europe . . . 22

of Lilly's Love's Metamorphosis, by Collier . . . 23

of Marston's Antonio and Mellida, by Bullen . . . 27

of Warwick's Spare Minutes, in Retrospective Review . . 34

Criticisms on Latin and English authors in Ascham's Scholemaster . 7

PAGE

Criticisms on Lives of Duke and Duchess of Newcastle . . . 30
Cromwell, Oliver, Wither fought for 41
Crowley, Robert, and authorship of Vision of Piers Ploughman . . 23
Crumms Fal'n from King James's Table, by Overbury . . . 31
Cupid's Triumph, in Hazlitt's Poetry of England 19
Cure for a Cuckold, by Webster . 38
Cursing, Sir John Rowll's, in Hazlitt's Poetry of Scotland . . 16

DANE HEW, Mery Jest of, in Hazlitt's Poetry of England . . 19
Daniel, Samuel, praises Chapman's translation of Homer . . . 13
Darby, Countesse Dowager of, Lorde and Ladye Huntingdon's Entertainment of, by Marston . . 40
Davenant, Sir William, Carew's Cœlum Britannicum attributed to 11
Cruel Brother, Wither said to be original of Castruccio in . 41
Day-Fatality of Rome, by Pell, in Aubrey's Miscellanies . . . 8
Day-Fatality; or, Some Observations on Days Lucky and Unlucky, by Aubrey 8
Days, Book of, by Hesiod, translated by Chapman 12
Debate and Stryfe betwene Somer and Wynter, in Hazlitt's Poetry of England 19
Debate of the Carpenters Tools, in Hazlitt's Poetry of England . 19
Decker, Thomas, Famous History of Sir Thomas Wyat, by Webster and 40
North-VVard Hoe, by Webster and 39
VVest-VVard Hoe, by Webster and 40
Denham, Sir John, saves Wither from hanging 42

PAGE

Dennis, John, uses story of Webster's Appius 38
Deo Opt. Max., a Poem, by Sandys . 33
Derby, Countess Dowager of, Lorde and Ladye Huntingdon's Entertainment of, by Marston . . 40
Descriptioun of Pedder Coffeis, in Hazlitt's Poetry of Scotland . . 16
Deuil's Law-case, by Webster . . 39
Devonshire, Duke of, possesses unique original of Webster's Monuments of Honor 39
Dibdin, T. F., amusing note on Hearne in his Bibliomania . 21
early editions of La Mort d'Arthure described by . . 25
Dickers, Thomas, see Decker.
Dilke, C. W., Marston's What You Will in Old Plays of . . . 29
Discontented Colonel, first title of Suckling's Brennoralt . . . 36
Disraeli, Isaac, on Camden, in his Calamities 10
Divine Poem of Musæus, The, translated by Chapman . . . 12
Doctour doubble ale, in Hazlitt's Poetry of England . ' . . 19
Don Quixote, Amadis of Gaul one of the three romances spared by the curate in 25
Dorset, Duke of, see Sackville, Charles.
Dorset, Earl of, see Sackville, Thomas.
Drayton, Michael, Complete Works, unfinished 14
friend of Drummond of Hawthornden 15
Harmonie of the Church . . 15
destroyed by public order 15
metrical rendering of parts of the Scriptures . . 15
unique copy in the British Museum . . . 15
memoir of, promised in his works 14

Drayton, Michael, Nymphydia an inspiration to Herrick . . 15
Poly-Olbion 14
criticised by Ellis . . 14
versified guide-book to Great Britain 14
portrait of, in his Works . . 14
Song of Salomon considered the best part of his Harmonie . 15
Dreame, Ane Godlie, in Hazlitt's Poetry of Scotland . . . 16
Dreams, in Aubrey's Miscellanies . 8
Dreme, Lichtoun's, in Hazlitt's Poetry of Scotland 16
Drummond, William, of Hawthornden, description of . . 15
Drayton and Jonson friends of . 15
furnishes men to fight against Charles I. 15
grieves at death of Charles I. . 15
Poetical Works . . . 15
Polemo-Middinia, authorship in doubt 15
sonnets commended . . . 15
verse written to Charles I. . 15
Dryden, John, Sandys's poetry eulogized by 34
Duik of Orlyance, etc., in Hazlitt's Poetry of Scotland . . . 16
Dutch Courtezan, The, by Marston . 27
Dyce, Alexander, first to reprint Webster's Sir Thomas Wyat . 40
omissions in his edition of Webster's Works 38
says John Webster did not write Thracian Wonder . . . 40
writes of Webster's North-VVard and VVestward Hoe . . 39

EARLY English Text Society publishes Skeat's edition of Piers Ploughman 23
Early Metrical Tales, by Laing, included in Early Popular Poetry of Scotland 16

Eastward Hoe, by Chapman, Jonson, and Marston 27
causes the imprisonment of its authors 27
Ebsworth, J. W., Carew's Poems edited by 11
condemns Dr. Jessopp's criticism of Carew . . . 11
Ecclesiastes, Paraphrase upon, by Sandys 33
Ecstacy, in Aubrey's Miscellanies . 8
Edward VI., Ascham secretary to . 6
Egyngecourte, Batayle of, in Hazlitt's Poetry of England . . 19
Egypt, Sandys travelled in . . 34
Eikon Basilike, 1649, includes Suckling's Coppy of a Letter found at Whitehall 37
Elegie vpon the Death of Sir Iohn Sutlin 37
Elegies by Overbury . . . 31
in Overbury's " Wife" . . 32
on Henry, Prince of Wales, Webster's Monumental Columne one of three 39
Elizabeth, Queen, appoints Sackville to announce her execution to Mary, Queen of Scots . . 32
Ascham tutor and secretary to . 6
Ellis, George, on Drayton's Poly-Olbion 14
praises Wither's writings . . 41
Emblems, Wither best known for his 42
Emerson, R. W., an admirer of Chapman 13
Enchiridion of Quarles . . . 32
Endimion, by Lilly . . . 23
England, Drayton's Poly-Olbion a versified guide-book to . . 14
Early Popular Poetry of, by Hazlitt 18
Roman Catholic priests in, under Elizabeth 35
English country life, old, in Herrick's Hesperides 22

INDEX

PAGE

English prose composition improved
by Ascham's Toxophilus . 7
schools and Greek pronunciation 7
writers criticised in Ascham's
Scholemaster . . . 7
Epigrams in Camden's Remains . 10
of Homer, translated by Chap-
man 12
Epistill of the Hermeit, etc., in Haz-
litt's Poetry of Scotland . . 16
Epistles, Ascham's, criticised in Ful-
ler's Worthies 6
Epitaph of Jack Puffe, in Hazlitt's
Poetry of England . . . 18
Epitaphs in Camden's Remains 9, 10
Essex, Countess of, see Somerset,
Countess of.
Estmere, King, in Hazlitt's Poetry of
Scotland 17
Eubulus, his lengthy remark, in Sack-
ville's Ferrex and Porrex . . 33
Euphuist, John Lilly, the . . 23
Extra Poems from Manuscripts attrib-
uted to Carew 11

FAC-SIMILE title-page of Love-
lace's Lucasta, first edition . 25
title-page of Wither's Hale-
luiah 40
of Wither's Hymns . . 41
title-pages in Hazlitt's Poetry of
England . . . 18
Fairholt, F. W., Lilly's Dramatic
Works edited by . . . 23
on Lilly's plays . . . 23
Fair Lady of Faguell, in Hazlitt's
Poetry of England . . . 19
Farr, Edward, writes Introduction to
Wither's works . . . 40, 41
Fatalities of Families and Places, in
Aubrey's Miscellanies . . . 8
Fatal Secret, by Theobald, adapted
from Webster's Duchess of Malfi . 39
Fawne : Parasitaster; or, The, by
Marston 28

PAGE

Fermorar and his Dochter, The, in
Hazlitt's Poetry of Scotland . . 16
Ferrers, George, Myrroure for Magis-
trates completed by Baldwin and . 33
Ferrex and Porrex, by Sackville . 33
Finch, Lord, in Suckling's Four Fu-
gitives Meeting 37
Four Fugitives Meeting, by Suckling 37
Free Library of Philadelphia has
Sommer's edition of La Mort d'Ar-
thure 26
Frere and the Boye, in Hazlitt's Poe-
try of England 19
Frogs and Mise, Homer's Batracho-
myomachia; or, the Battaile of . 12
Fuller, Thomas, on Ascham . . 6

GAIST, The Laying of Lord Fer-
gus's, in Hazlitt's Poetry of Scot-
land 16
Galaunt, A Treatise of a, in Hazlitt's
Poetry of England . . . 19
Gallathea, by Lilly 23
Games, May-day, described in Her-
rick's Hesperides 22
Gardening, Spence's home amuse-
ment 35
Georgics of Hesiod, translated by
Chapman 12
Germany, affairs and state of, by As-
cham 5
Ascham's visit to . . . 5
Gibbon, Edward, sneers at Hearne . 21
Gibbons, Orlando, composes tunes for
Wither's Hymns 42
Giles, Rev. Dr. J. A., Life of As-
cham, in his Works . . 5
on Works of Ascham . . 5
Glances of Love and Malice, in Au-
brey's Miscellanies . . . 8
Glasse to Viewe the Pride of Women,
in Hazlitt's Poetry of England . 19
Glassinberry, a poem by, in Hazlitt's
Poetry of Scotland . . . 16

INDEX

PAGE

Glossarial Index to Chapman's
Works 12
Glossary, in Hazlitt's Poetry of Scot-
land 16
in Langland's Piers Ploughman 22
of old words, in Ascham's Let-
ters *and* Toxophilus . 6, 7
Glyn, Miss Isabella, acts in Web-
ster's Duchess of Malfi . . 39
Goblins, The, by Suckling . . 37
Godlie Dreame, Ane, in Hazlitt's
Poetry of Scotland . . . 16
Gorboduc, Sackville's Ferrex and
Porrex surreptitiously printed as . 33
Gossip in Hearne's Remains . . 21
Graces said at Oxford Colleges, in
Hearne's Remains . . . 21
Grant, Edward, a friend of Ascham
and Camden 6
Oration on Life and Death of
Ascham 6
Great Britain, Drayton's Poly-Olbion
a versified guide-book to . 14
first macaronic poem by native of 15
Greece, Sandys travelled in . . 34
Greek and Latin, Ascham's Toxo-
philus a protest against the exclu-
sive study of 7
Greek, English pronunciation of, in-
troduced by Sir John Cheke . . 7
Gregory Nazianzen, St., Χριστὸς
Πάσχων attributed to . . . 34
Grosart, A. B., edition of Crashaw's
poems by 14
Grotius, Hugh, Christus Patiens,
translated by Sandys . . . 34
Guide-book in verse, Drayton's Poly-
Olbion so called 14
Gyre-Carling, The, in Hazlitt's Poetry
of Scotland 16

Hales, John, his gossip about
Thomas Carew 11
Hales, J. W., on Creed of Piers
Ploughman 22

PAGE

Hall, Dr. Joseph, ridicules Southwell's poems 35
Hallam, Henry, commends Drummond's sonnets . . . 15
his choice of Overbury's Characters 31
on Amadis of Gaul in Literature of Europe . . . 24
on Herrick in Literature of Europe 22
Hallelujah; or, Britain's Second Remembrancer, by Wither . . 40
Halliwell-Phillipps, J. O., notes to
Marston's Works by . . . 26
Harlaw, The Battle of, in Hazlitt's
Poetry of Scotland . . . 16
Harvard College, Increase Mather
president of 30
Hawthornden, William Drummond
of, *see* Drummond.
Hazlitt, William, commends Drum-
mond's Sonnets . . . 15
on authorship of The Malcon-
tent 39
praises Lilly 24
Webster's Dramatic Works ed-
ited by 38
Hazlitt, W. Carew, Early Popular
Poetry of Scotland edited by . 16
Herrick's Hesperides edited by . 22
Lovelace's Lucasta edited by . 25
Remains of the Early Popular
Poetry of England . . 18
Hearne, Thomas, amusing note on,
in Dibdin's Bibliomania . 21
appointed to post in Bodleian
library 21
Bibliotheca Hearniana, in his
Remains 21
Gibbon sneers at . . . 21
graces said at Oxford colleges
recorded by 21
note-book carried constantly by . 21
observations on Pope in his Re-
mains 21

INDEX

PAGE

Hearne, Thomas, old English chronicles edited by . . . 21

pilloried by Pope in the Dunciad 21

Reliquiæ Hearnianæ: the Remains of 21

Sally Salisbury in his Remains . 21

Whipping Stories in his Remains 21

Henry VIII., Ascham's Toxophilus dedicated to. 7

Hereford, Walter Brute persecuted at 22

Hermeit of Alareit, in Hazlitt's Poetry of Scotland. 16

Hero and Leander of Musæus translated by Chapman . . . 12

Herrick, Robert, applies to his uncle for money 22

descriptions of old English country life by 22

Drayton's Nymphidia an inspiration to 15

Hesperides: the Poems and Remains of 22

Memoir and portrait of, in Hesperides 22

poems withdrawn from the last edition of Hesperides . . 22

writings reviewed by Hallam . 22

Herrick, Sir William, letters from Robert Herrick to . . . 22

Hesiod, translated by Cooke, 1728 . 12

Works and Days, translated by Chapman 12

Works gave idea of Georgics to Virgil 12

Hesperides: the Poems and Remains of Robert Herrick . . . 22

Heywood, Thomas, writes one of Three Elegies on the Death of Prince Henrie . . . 39

History of a Lord, etc., in Hazlitt's Poetry of Scotland . . . 16

History of Sir Eger, etc., in Hazlitt's Poetry of Scotland . . . 16

History of Tom Thumb, in Hazlitt's Poetry of England . . . 19

PAGE

Holy Land, Sandys travelled in . 34

Homer, Batrachomyomachia, translated by Chapman . . . 12

Chapman's description of Iliad and Odyssey 13

Hymns and Epigrams, translated by Chapman 12

Iliads, translated by Chapman . 13

Odysseys, translated by Chapman 13

translation by Chapman a great achievement 13

Hooper, Rev. Richard, Introductions and Notes to Chapman's Works . . . 12, 13

to Drayton's Works . . 14

to Sandys's Works . . 33

on Chapman's life . . . 14

Horsemanship, System of, Duke of Newcastle best known by his . 31

How a Merchande dyd hys Wyfe Betray, in Hazlitt's Poetry of England 19

How a Sergeaunt wolde lerne to be a Frere, in Poetry of England . 19

How the Goode Wif Thaught hir Doughter, in Hazlitt's Poetry of England 19

How the Plowman Lerned his Pater Noster, in Poetry of England . 19

How the Wise Man Taught his Son, in Poetry of England . . . 19

Hydriotaphia: Urn-Burial, by Sir Thomas Browne . . . 7, 9

Hye Way to the Spyttel Hous, in Hazlitt's Poetry of England . . 19

Hymn to the Nativity, by Milton, indebted to Crashaw . . . 14

Hymns and Songs of the Church, by Wither 41

in Drayton's Harmonie of the Church 15

in Wither's Hallelujah . . 40

of Homer, translated by Chapman 11

INDEX

ILIAD of Homer and Chapman's
translations 12, 13
Impresses, in Camden's Remains . 9
Impulses, in Aubrey's Miscellanies . 8
Induction to the Myrroure for Magistrates, by Sackville . . 33
to The Malcontent, by Webster 39
Injured Love, by Tate, a reprint of
Webster's White Divel . . 40
Inquisition in Spain, in Newes from
Sir John Sucklin 37
Insatiate Countesse, by Marston . 28
Institutions, Divine and Moral, in
Quarles's Enchiridion . . . 32
Italianated Englishmen attacked in
Ascham's Scholemaster . . 7
Italy, Ascham makes tour of . . 7
Sandys travelled in . . . 34
Itinerary of Leland improved upon
by Camden's Britannia . . 10

JACK PUFFE, in Hazlitt's Poetry
of England 19
James I., Carr a favourite of . . 31
offended by Eastward Hoe, imprisons Chapman and Marston 27
Scotch accent mimicked on the
stage 27
suspected of complicity in Overbury's poisoning . . . 31
Jeremiah, Lamentations of, Sandys's
Paraphrase upon 33
Jesse, J. H., on passage in Marston's
Eastward Hoe 27
Jessopp, Augustus, article on Carew
criticised by Ebsworth . . . 11
Jesus, Society of, Southwell received
into 35
Job, Sandys's Paraphrase upon . 33
John I. of Portugal knights Lobeira 24
John Bon and Mast Person, in Hazlitt's Poetry of England . . 19
John the Reeve, in Hazlitt's Poetry
of Scotland 16

Johnson, Dr. Samuel, on Selden's
Table-Talk 34
uses particulars from Spence's
Anecdotes 36
Jok and Jynny, The Wowing of, in
Hazlitt's Poetry of Scotland . 16
Jones, Inigo, the masque invented by
Carew and 11
Jonson, Ben, a friend of Drummond's 15
and Marston quarrel frequently 26
Eastward Hoe, by Chapman,
Marston, and . . . 27
his high estimate of Lilly . . 24
joins Marston and Chapman in
prison 27
Marston dedicates The Malcontent to 28
praise of Chapman's translation
of Homer 13
satirizes Marston in the Poetaster 26
Justes of the Moneths of May and
June, in Hazlitt's Poetry of England 19
Juvenal, fifth satire of, translated by
Chapman as A Just Reproofe of a
Romane Smell-Feast . . . 12

KEATS, JOHN, an admirer of
Chapman's Homer . . . 13
King and a Poore Northerne Man, in
Hazlitt's Poetry of England . 19
and the Barker, in Poetry of
England. 19
Berdok, in Hazlitt's Poetry of
Scotland 16
Estmere, in Poetry of Scotland . 17
James the Sext, The Promine to,
in Poetry of Scotland . . 17
Lear, altered by Tate, who dubs
himself its "author" . 40
lines from, in Suckling's
Goblins 37
Orfeo, etc., in Hazlitt's Poetry
of Scotland 17

Kinsayder, W., pseudonym of Marston 28

Knight of Curtesy, in Hazlitt's Poetry of England 19

Knights of the Round Table in Malory's La Mort d'Arthure . . . 25

Knockings, in Aubrey's Miscellanies 8

Knowles, Sheridan, uses story of Webster's Appius . . . 38

Knyght and his Wyfe, in Hazlitt's Poetry of England . . . 19

K., W., initials used by Marston . 28

Kyng and the Hermyt, in Hazlitt's Poetry of England . . . 19

Kynge Roberd of Cysille, in Hazlitt's Poetry of England . . 18, 19

LAING, DAVID, Ancient Popular Poetry of Scotland, by, included in Early Popular Poetry of Scotland 16

Early Metrical Tales, included in Early Popular Poetry of Scotland 16

Lamb, Charles, finds much to praise in Wither's writings . . 41

estimate of the Duchess of Newcastle 31

opinion of the Lives of the Duke and Duchess of Newcastle . 30

praise of Chapman's translation of Homer 13

praises Lilly 24

Lamentations of Jeremiah, Sandys's Paraphrase upon 33

Langbaine, Gerard, on Marston's What You Will 29

Langland, Robert, once supposed to be author of Piers Ploughman . 23

Langland, William, authorship of the Creed of Piers Ploughman in doubt 23

Church only attacked by the "Creed," the "Vision" attacks Church and State . . 23

Langland, William, Malvern Hills connected with the Vision of Piers Ploughman . . . 23

occupied thirty years in writing the "Vision" . . . 23

Professor Hales on the Creed of Piers Ploughman . . . 22

texts of the "Vision" published by the Early English Text Society 23

Vision and Creed of Piers Ploughman . . . 22, 23

Wycliffe's opinions approved by the "Creed" . . . 22

Language, vernacular, and Ascham's Toxophilus 7

Languages, in Camden's Remains .. 9

Latin and Greek, Ascham's Toxophilus against the exclusive study of 7

Latin, Camden's Britannia published in 9

ludicrous use of, in Drummond's Polemo-Middinia . . . 15

method of learning, in Ascham's Scholemaster . . . 7

Latin Poems of Ascham . . . 6

Lawes, Henry, sets Carew's Cœlum Britannicum to music . . 11

tunes for Psalms of David, in Sandys's Poetical Works . 33

Laying of Lord Fergus's Gaist, in Hazlitt's Poetry of England . . 17

Legends, in Myrroure for Magistrates 33

Lekeux, Lord, in Newes from Sir John Sucklin 37

Leland's Itinerary improved upon by Camden's Britannia . . . 10

Letter sent by Sir Iohn Suckling from France 37

Letters of Herrick to his uncle, in Hesperides 22

of Roger Ascham . . . 6

Seven, of Giles Ascham . . 6

INDEX

Library of Old Authors, general title 5
sold to Mr. Reeves for £1000 . 5
Lichtoun's Dreme, in Hazlitt's Poetry
of Scotland 17
Lillian, Roswall and, in Hazlitt's Po-
etry of Scotland 17
Lilly, John, Blount's description of . 24
Campaspe, in Dramatic Works . 23
Collier criticises Love's Meta-
morphosis 23
Dramatic Works . . . 23
Endimion, in Dramatic Works . 23
first work the Woman in the
Moone 24
Gallathea, in Dramatic Works . 23
Jonson ranks him before Kyd or
Marlowe 24
life of, in Dramatic Works . 23
Love's Metamorphosis, in Dra-
matic Works . . . 23
Maid's Metamorphosis not by . 23
Man in the Moone, second title
to Endimion 23
Mother Bombie, in Dramatic
Works 23
Mydas, in Dramatic Works . 24
Pliny's Natural History furnishes
subject for Campaspe . . 23
praised by various writers . . 24
Sapho and Phao, in Dramatic
Works 24
success as a dramatist . . 24
two plays omitted from present
edition 23
Warning for Faire Women not
by 23
Woman in the Moone, in Dramatic Works . . . 24
might have suggested idea
of Midsummer Night's
Dream 24
"wonderful beliefs" as to animals in Mydas 24
Livy, Marston's Wonder of Women
founded on 29

Lobeira, Vasco de, Amadis of Gaul,
translated by Southey . 24
description of . . 24, 25
spared by the curate in Don
Quixote 24
date of death variously given . 24
receives knighthood from King
John of Portugal . . . 24
London, Lovelace dies in Gunpowder Alley 25
London Stone and the fayre pusell,
in Poetry of England . . . 19
Longfellow, H. W., praises Lilly . 24
Longland, William, see Langland.
Lord and His Three Sons, in Hazlitt's Poetry of Scotland . . 17
Lorde and Ladye Huntingdon's Entertainement of their Mother, etc.,
by Marston 28
Lovelace, Richard, is " Alexis" in
his Amarantha . . . 25
Lucasta: the poems of . . 25
Lucy Sacheverell his "Ama-
"rantha" and "Lucasta" . 25
memoir and portrait of, in Lu-
casta 25
two best reputed poems of . 25
Lovers Quarrel, in Hazlitt's Poetry
of England 19
in Hazlitt's Poetry of Scotland . 17
Love's Metamorphosis, by Lilly . 23
Lowell, J. R., on Southwell's St. Pe-
ter's Complaint 35
Lower, M.A., edits Lives of the Duke
and Duchess of Newcastle . . 30
Lucasta, by Lovelace . . . 25
Lux Casta, Lovelace calls Lucy
Sacheverell his 25
Lyfe of Roberte the Deuyll, in Hazlitt's Poetry of England . 18, 19
Lyly, John, see Lilly.

MAGICK, in Aubrey's Miscellanies 8

INDEX

PAGE

Magistrates, Myrroure for, planned by Sackville 33

Magnalia of Cotton Mather among the most important of his writings 29

Maidin, The Murning, in Hazlitt's Poetry of Scotland . . . 17

Maid's Metamorphosis not by Lilly . 23

Malcontent, The, by Marston and Webster 28, 39

Malfy, Tragedy of the Dutchess of, by Webster 39

Malone, Edmund, edition of Spence's Anecdotes by . . . 35

praises Lilly 24

uses original MS. of Spence's Anecdotes for his Life of Dryden 36

Malory, Sir Thomas, La Mort d'Arthure, edited by Wright . 25

Sommer's edition in Free Library of Philadelphia 26

various editions of . 25, 26

Malvern Hills, Vision of Piers Ploughman connected with . . 23

Manchester, Eng., Althorp collection property of city of . . . 26

Mandevelle, Ser John, Commonyng of and the Gret Souden, in Hazlitt's Poetry of England . . 19

Maner of the Crying of Ane Playe, in Hazlitt's Poetry of Scotland . 17

Man in the Moone, second title of Lilly's Endimion . . . 23

significance of the phrase . . 23

Marriage, Selden's opinion of . . 34

Sir T. Browne on Women and . 9

Marston, John, and Jonson quarrel frequently 26

anecdote of 26

Antonio and Mellida, by . . 26

Antonio's Revenge, in his Works 27

Bullen's criticism on Antonio's Revenge, etc. . . . 27

City Pageant on Visit of King of Denmark 27

PAGE

Marston, John, dedicates Scourge of Villanie to himself . . 28

Dutch Courtezan, in his Works 27

Eastward Hoe, by Chapman, Jonson, and 27

imprisoned for writing Eastward Hoe 27

Insatiate Countesse, in his Works 28

James I. offended by reflections on the Scots in Eastward Hoe 27

Langbaine's criticism of What You Will 29

life and writings, account of, in his Works 26

Lorde and Ladye Huntingdon's Entertainement, etc., in his Works 28

Malcontent, The, by Webster and 28, 39

manners of, not commendable . 26

manuscript of City Pageant in the British Museum . . 27

Metamorphosis of Pigmalion's Image, etc., in his Works . 28

Order for Conflagration of his Pigmalion and Scourge of Villanie 28

Parasitaster; or, the Fawne, in his Works 28

pseudonym of " W. Kinsayder" assumed by 28

Revenge, The, revival by Betterton of his Dutch Courtezan 27

satirized by Jonson . . . 26

Scourge of Villanie, in his Works 28

Verses from Chester's Loves Martyr, in his Works . . 28

What You Will, in his Works . 29

Wonder of Women; or, The Tragedy of Sophonisba, by . 29

Works of, edited by Halliwell 26-29

Maryage of London Stone and the fayre pusell, in Hazlitt's Poetry of England 19

PAGE

Maryage, The Payne and Sorowe of Evyll, in Poetry of England . 19

Mary Magdalen's Tears, poem by Southwell 35

Mary, Queen, Ascham secretary to . 6

coronation of, in Webster's Wyat 40

Mary, Queen of Scots, anagram on, in Camden's Remains . . 10

Sackville selected to announce execution to 32

Masque, A, by Carew, . . . 11

Massachusetts, scene of Mather's Wonders of the Invisible World . 29

Massinger, Philip, Parliament of Love and Webster's Cure for a Cuckold 38

Massinissa, in Marston's Wonder of Women 29

Mather, Cotton, and the Witchcraft delusion in Massachusetts . 29

motto, " Be short" . . . 30

published 382 pieces during lifetime 29

Wonders of the Invisible World, by 29

Mather family charged with witchcraft 29

Mather, Increase, aids his son Cotton in attacking witchcraft . . 30

Further Account of the Tryals of the New-England Witches, by 29

president of Harvard College, 1684-1701 30

refuses to conform after the Restoration and comes to America 30

Remarkable Providences, by . 30

Matrymonie, Ane Ballat of, in Hazlitt's Poetry of Scotland . . 17

Maundeville, Sir John, in Hazlitt's Poetry of England . . . 18

May and June, Justes of the Moneths of, in Poetry of England . . 19

Mayd Emlyn, The Boke of, in Poetry of England . . . 19

PAGE

May, Welcum to, in Hazlitt's Poetry of Scotland 17

Merchant and his Son, The, in Hazlitt's Poetry of England . . 19

Merry Ieste of a Shrewde and Curste Wyfe, etc. 19

Mery Geste, How the Plowman Lerned his Pater Noster . . 19

Mery Geste of the Frere and the Boye 19

Mery Jest how a Sergeaunt wolde lerne to be a Frere 20

Mery Jest of Dane Hew, Munk of Leicestre 20

Mery Jest of the Mylner of Abyngton 20

Metamorphosis of Pigmalion's Image, by Marston 28

Middlesex, Earl of, and Joseph Spence 35

Milton, John, in many passages indebted to Crashaw . . . 14

Milward, Richard, compiles Selden's Table-Talk 34

Miranda, in Aubrey's Miscellanies . 8

Mirror for Magistrates, planned by Sackville 33

Miscellanies upon Various Subjects, by Aubrey 7

Moncrieff, John, uses story of Webster's Appius 38

Moneys, in Camden's Remains, . 9

Monumental Columne to the Prince of Wales, by Webster . . . 39

Monuments of Honor, by Webster . 39

Moralities, by Spence . . . 35

Morley, Henry, describes Lovelace . 25

Mort d'Arthure, by Malory . . 25

Mother Bombie, by Lilly . . . 23

Motto of Cotton Mather, " Be short". 30

Murning Maidin, The, in Hazlitt's Poetry of Scotland . . . 17

Musæus, Hero and Leander, translated by Chapman . . . 12

unique original of Chapman's translation of, in the Bodleian 12

	PAGE
Musarum Deliciæ, Suckling's Aglaura ridiculed in	36
Music, Sandys's Psalms of David set to	33
Mydas, in Lilly's Dramatic Works	24
Mylner of Abyngton, Mery Jest of, in Hazlitt's Poetry of England	20
Myrroure for Magistrates, planned by Sackville	33

	PAGE
NAMES, in Camden's Remains	9
Nepos, Cornelius, Marston's What You Will founded on	29
Newcastle, Henry, second Duke of, Spence tutor to	35
Newcastle, Lives of Duke and Duchess of, edited by Lower	30
Lamb's opinion of	30
various criticisms of	30, 31
New England witch trials, in Cotton Mather's Wonders of the Invisible World	29
in Increase Mather's Further Account, etc.	29
Newes from any Whence, by Overbury	31
Newes from Sir John Sucklin	37
New Newes, in Overbury's "Wife"	32
New Nutborne Mayd, etc., in Hazlitt's Poetry of England	20
Noble Numbers, in Herrick's Hesperides	22
Nobles, Ane Ballet of Nine, in Hazlitt's Poetry of Scotland	17
Norris, William, supposed writer of Suckling's Letter from France	37
North American Review on Mather's Remarkable Providences	30
North-VVard Hoe, by Decker and Webster	39
title a cry of the Thames watermen	39
Notbrowne Mayde, The, in Hazlitt's Poetry of England	20

	PAGE
Note-books carried constantly by Hearne	21
Notes and Queries on Suckling's Letter from France	37
publishes "Order for Conflagration" of Marston's books	28
Nutborne Mayd, The New, etc., in Hazlitt's Poetry of England	20
Nymphidia of Drayton, an inspiration to Herrick	15

	PAGE
ODES, in Webster's Dramatic Works	39
Odysseys of Homer, translated by Chapman	13
Offor, George, Introduction to Mather's Remarkable Providences	30
Omens, in Aubrey's Miscellanies	8
Oracles, in Aubrey's Miscellanies	8
Oration on the Life and Death of Ascham, by Grant	6
Orfeo and Heurodis, in Hazlitt's Poetry of Scotland	17
Oriana and Amadis, in Lobeira's Amadis of Gaul	24
Orlyance, the Duik of, in Hazlitt's Poetry of Scotland	17
Ostenta, or Portents, in Aubrey's Miscellanies	8
Overbury, Sir Thomas, biographical account of, in his Works	31
Characters, in his Works	31
Crumms Fal'n from King James's Table	31
Elegies	31
friendship with Carr, Earl of Somerset	31
Miscellaneous Works of	31
murder of, wrapped up in mystery	31
Newes from any Whence, etc.	31
New Newes, etc., in his "Wife"	32
Remedy of Love, a paraphrase from Ovid	31

INDEX

Overbury, Sir Thomas, The XVII.
Provinces as They Stood
A.D. 1609 . · . . 32
tries to prevent the marriage of
Somerset to the Countess of
Essex 31, 32
Wife, in his Works . . . 32
Ovid paraphrased in Overbury's
Remedy of Love 31
Oxford, graces of colleges at, in Re-
liquiæ Hearnianæ . . 21
Selden's library presented to . 34
Spence succeeds Warton at . 35

PAINTER, WILLIAM, Palace of
Pleasure and Marston's Dutch
Courtezan 27
Marston's Insatiate Countesse
taken from 28
Webster's Appius a dramatiza-
tion of fifth novel of . . 38
Paradise Lost, Milton indebted to
Crashaw in 14
Parasitaster; or, The Fawne, by
Marston 28
Parlament of Byrdes, The, in Haz-
litt's Poetry of England . . 20
Paschal, Rev. Dr., Transportation by
an Invisible Power, in Aubrey's
Miscellanies 8
Pater Noster, Proude Wyues, in Haz-
litt's Poetry of England . . 20
Payne and Sorowe of Evyll Maryage 20
Pedder Coffeis, in Hazlitt's Poetry of
Scotland 17
Pell, Dr. John, Day-Fatality of Rome,
by, in Aubrey's Miscellanies . 8
Pension of £10 annually given to
Roger Ascham 7
Pepys, Samuel, on Lives of Duke
and Duchess of Newcastle . . 30
Percy, Thomas (Bishop), praises
Lilly 24
Phelps, Samuel, produces Webster's
Dutchesse of Malfy . . . 39

Phesoj Enceps, anagram of Joseph
Spence 35
Philadelphia, Free Library of, has
Sommer's edition of Morte
d'Arthur 26
Webster's Tragedy of Dutchesse
of Malfy produced in . . 39
Philip, King, in Webster's Sir
Thomas Wyat 40
Philologus, character in Ascham's
Toxophilus 7
identified with Sir John Cheke . 7
Piece of Friar Bacons Brazen-heads
Prophesie, in Hazlitt's Poetry of
England 20
Piers of Fullham, in Hazlitt's Poetry
of England 20
Piers Ploughman, Vision and Creed
of, by Langland 22
Pigmalion's Image, Metamorphosis
of, by Marston 28
Plagiarism by Suckling in his Bren-
noralt 36
Plato, discussion on, in Ascham's
Scholemaster 7
Plautus, Amphitruo, Marston's What
You Will copied from . . . 29
Playe, The Maner of the Crying of
Ane, in Hazlitt's Poetry of Scotland 17
Pliny's Natural History supplies sub-
ject of Lilly's Campaspe . . 23
Poem by Glassinberry, in Hazlitt's
Poetry of Scotland . . . 17
Poesies, in Camden's Remains . . 9
Poetry of England, Remains of Early
Popular, by Hazlitt . . 18
of Scotland, Early Popular, by
Hazlitt 16
Pieces of Ancient Popular, by
Ritson, included in Hazlitt's
Popular Poetry of England . 18
Polemo-Middinia, in Drummond's
Poetical Works 15
Politics, main interest of Sackville's
life 32

59

PAGE

Poly-Olbion, by Drayton . . . 14
Pope, Alexander, avails himself of
    lines from Crashaw . . 14
    copies Carew 11
    describes Wither in his Dunciad 41
    his admiration for Thomas Carew 11
    in Spence's Anecdotes . 35, 36
    Observations on, in Hearne's
    Remains 21
    pillories Hearne in his Dunciad 21
    praise of Chapman's translation
    of Homer 13
    Sandys's poetry eulogized by . 34
Pope, Mrs. A. E., pays £1950 for
    only complete copy of Caxton's
    Morte d'Arthur 26
Poppæa, mistress of Nero, in Juve-
    nal's Fifth Satire 12
Pore Helpe, A, in Hazlitt's Poetry of
    England 20
Portents, in Aubrey's Miscellanies . 8
Portrait of Drayton, in his Works . 14
    of Hearne, in Reliquiæ Hear-
    nianæ 21
    of Herrick, in his Hesperides . 22
    of Lovelace, in his Lucasta . 25
    of Margaret, Duchess of New-
    castle, in her Lives, etc. . 30
    of Sandys, in his Works . . 33
    of Spence, in his Anecdotes . 35
    of Suckling, in his Poems . 36
Predictions, etc., in Aubrey's Miscel-
    lanies 8
Priests of Peblis, in Hazlitt's Poetry
    of Scotland 17
Promine to King James the Sext, in
    Hazlitt's Poetry of Scotland . 17
Prophesies, in Aubrey's Miscellanies 8
Proude Wyue's Pater Noster, in Haz-
    litt's Poetry of England . . 20
Proverbs, in Camden's Remains 9, 10
Provinces, The XVII., in Over-
    bury's Miscellanies . . . 32
Psalms of David, Sandys's Para-
    phrase upon . . . 33

PAGE

Psalms, Paraphrase of Certain, by
    Carew 11
Pseudonyms, see Anonymity.
Pystyl of Swete Susan, in Hazlitt's
    Poetry of Scotland . . . 17

QUARLES, FRANCIS, Enchiri-
    dion 32
    praised by Thoreau . . 32
    reviewed in Restropective
    Review 32
Quene of Elf-Land, in Hazlitt's Poe-
    try of Scotland 17

RAGMAN ROLL, in Hazlitt's Poe-
    try of England 20
Raleigh, Sir Walter, History of the
    World, tragedy of Sophonisba in 29
Rauf Coilzear, Tale of, in Hazlitt's
    Poetry of Scotland . . 17
Ray, John, Collection of Proverbs
    suggested by Camden's Remains . 10
Rebuses, in Camden's Remains . 10
Reeve, John the, in Hazlitt's Poetry
    of Scotland 17
Reeves & Turner purchase Library
    of Old Authors 5
Religio Medici of Sir T. Browne con-
    tains curious views on women and
    marriage 9
Religion, An Account of, in Suck-
    ling's Poems, etc. . . . 38
Reliquiæ Hearnianæ: the Remains
    of Thomas Hearne . . . 21
Remains Concerning Britain, by
    Camden 9
Remarkable Providences, by Mather 30
Remedy of Love, by Overbury . 31
Report and Discourse of the Affaires
    and State of Germany, by Ascham 5
Retrospective Review, articles on
    Wither in 42
    on Ascham's Toxophilus . . 7
    on Warwick's Spare Minutes . 34

PAGE

Retrospective Review, Quarles's Enchiridion reviewed in . . 32
Southwell's Poems subject of article in 35
Revenge, The, revival by Betterton of Marston's Dutch Courtezan . 27
Richard III., and Henry, Duke of Buckingham 33
Ridley, Rev. James, Tales of the Genii, Spence figures in . . 35
Rimbault, Dr. E. F., edits Overbury's Works 31
Ring of the Roy Robert, in Hazlitt's Poetry of Scotland . . . 17
Ritson, Joseph, Pieces of Ancient Popular Poetry included in Hazlitt's Popular Poetry of England . 18
Roane, Dr., in Suckling's Four Fugitives Meeting . . . 37
Roberd of Cysille, Kynge, in Hazlitt's Poetry of England . . 18, 19
Roberte the Deuyll, Lyfe of, in Hazlitt's Poetry of England . . 18, 20
Robin Conscience, Booke of, in Hazlitt's Poetry of England . . 20
Rochester, Viscount, see Somerset, Earl of.
Rolls Series and Hearne's editions of old English chronicles . . . 21
Rome, Day-Fatality of, in Aubrey's Miscellanies. 8
Rosalin's Complaint: Verses from Chester's Love's Martyr; or, by Marston 28
Rosamond of Scotland, in Hazlitt's Poetry of Scotland . . . 17
Roswall and Lillian, in Hazlitt's Poetry of Scotland . . . 17
Rowley, William, Cure for a Cuckold, by Webster and . . 38
Thracian Wonder, by John or William Webster and . . 40
Royalists deserted by Wither . . 42
Roy Robert, Ring of the, in Hazlitt's Poetry of Scotland, . . . 17

PAGE

Rutland, Countess of, attempted intrigue of Overbury with alluded to in his "Wife" 32

SACHEVERELL, LUCY, surmised to be "Lucasta" and "Amaran-"tha" in Lovelace's Poems . . 25
Sackville, Charles, second Duke of Dorset, employs Spence as tutor . 35
Sackville, Thomas, Earl of Dorset, Ferrex and Porrex by . 32, 33
Myrroure for Magistrates planned by 33
selected to announce her execution to Mary, Queen of Scots . 32
Works, edited by R. W. Sackville-West 32
wrote first English tragedy in blank verse 32
Sackville-West, R. W., Sackville's Works edited by 32
Sad One, The, by Suckling . . 38
St. Gregory Nazianzen, Χριστὸς πάσχων attributed to 34
Saint Peter's Complaint, Southwell's principal poem 35
St. Teresa, Crashaw's poem on, inspired second part of Christabel . 14
Salem Witchcraft, in Mather's Wonders of the Invisible World . . 29
Salisbury, Sally, in Hearne's Remains 21
Salomon, Song of, in Drayton's Harmonie of the Church . . . 15
Sandys, George, Christ's Passion translated from Grotius by . 33
Paraphrases upon Job, the Psalms, etc., by . . . 33
Poem, Deo Opt. Max., by . 33
Poetical Works, edited by Hooper 33
praised by Dr. Burney, Dryden, etc. 33, 34
Sapho and Phao, by Lilly . . 24

PAGE

Satires: Juvenal's Fifth Satyre, translated by Chapman . . . 12
Langland's Vision of Piers Ploughman 23
Marston's Metamorphosis of Pigmalions Image . . 28
Scourge of Villanie . . 28
Scaliger, Julius, epitaph on, in Camden's Remains 10
Schole-house of Women, in Hazlitt's Poetry of England . . . 20
Scholemaster, The, by Ascham . 6
Schole of Shootinge, Toxophilus, the, by Ascham 7
Scotland, Early Popular Poetry of, by Hazlitt 16
Second-Sighted Men in, in Aubrey's Miscellanies . . 8
Scots, Duik of Orlyance in Defence of the, in Hazlitt's Poetry of Scotland 17
Scots, Mary, Queen of, Sackville selected to announce execution to . 32
Scots, reflections on the, in Marston's Eastward Hoe 27
Scourge of Villanie, by Marston . 28
Scriptures metrically rendered in Drayton's Harmonie of the Church 15
Second-Sight, in Aubrey's Miscellanies 8
in Mather's Remarkable Providences. 30
Second-Sighted Men in Scotland, in Aubrey's Miscellanies . . . 8
Selden, John, his library presented to Oxford 34
on quotations and on marriage . 34
Table-Talk, with biography and notes by Singer . . . 34
used spectacles as book-marks . 34
Ser John Mandevelle, in Hazlitt's Poetry of England . . . 20
Session of the Poets, Suckling's best known piece. . . . 37
verses from . . . 11, 36

PAGE

Seven letters of Giles Ascham . . 6
Shakespeare, William, Chapman the rival poet referred to in his Sonnets 14
entire lines in Suckling's Brennoralt taken from . . . 36
idea of Suckling's Goblins borrowed from 37
Lilly praised in Jonson's verses on 24
Midsummer Night's Dream and Lilly's Woman in the Moone . 24
Suckling's admiration for . 36
Shrew, epitaph on a, from Camden's Remains 10
Shrewde and Curste Wyfe, A Mery Ieste of a, etc., in Hazlitt's Poetry of England 19
Singer, S. W., Biographical Notice of Herrick by . . . 22
Selden's Table-Talk edited by . 34
Spence's Anecdotes edited by . 35
Sir Eger, etc., History of, in Hazlitt's Poetry of Scotland . . . 17
Sir John Barleycorn, in Hazlitt's Poetry of Scotland . . . 17
Sir John Rowll's Cursing, in Hazlitt's Poetry of Scotland . . . 17
Skeat, W. W., edition of Piers Ploughman printed by Early English Text Society 23
Smith, John Russell, publishes Library of Old Authors . . 5
receives £1000 for Library of Old Authors 5
Smyth and his Dame, in Hazlitt's Poetry of England . . . 20
Solomon, Song of, Sandys's Paraphrase upon. 33
Somer and Wynter, Debate and Stryfe Betweene 20
Somerset, Countess of, and Sir Thomas Overbury . . 31, 32
Somerset, Robert Carr, Earl of, convicted of Overbury's poisoning . 31

Somerset, Robert Carr, Earl of, Overbury tries to prevent his marriage with the Countess of Essex 31, 32
Sonnet to, in Chapman's Iliads. 13
Sommer, Oskar, edition of Malory's Morte Darthur by. . . . 26
Song of Solomon, Sandys's Paraphrase upon. 33
Songs in Carew's Masque set to music 11
Songs of the Church, Hymns and, by Wither 41
Songs out of the Old and New Testaments, Sandys's Paraphrase upon . 33
Sonnets addressed to noble patrons, in Chapman's Homer's Iliads. 13
of Drummond commended . 15
Sophonisba, Marston's Wonder of Women; or, The Tragedie of . 29
Southey, Robert, Amadis of Gaul translated by . . . 24
praises Wither's writings . . 41
Southwell, Robert, criticisms of his poems 35
incidents in his life described . 35
Poetical Works, edited by Turnbull 35
Sow, Tale of Colkelbie, in Hazlitt's Poetry of Scotland . . . 17
Spare Minutes, by Warwick, in Selden's Table-Talk 34
Spectacles used as book-marks by Selden 34
Spence, Joseph, anagram of Phesoj Enceps on 35
Anecdotes, Observations, and Characters, edited by Singer . 35
author of Moralities, and Crito, a dialogue 35
described in Ridley's Tales of the Genii 35
editions of his Anecdotes described 35
Life and portrait of . . . 35

Spence, Joseph, literary history of the 18th century in his Anecdotes 35, 36
pseudonym of "Sir Harry Beaumont" used by . . . 35
succeeded Warton at Oxford . 35
Spencer, Earl, acquires copy of Morte d'Arthur for £325 . . 26
Althorp collection now owned by the city of Manchester . 26
Spirit-Rapping, in Mather's Remarkable Providences 30
Sports, Herrick noted for descriptions of old English 22
Spyttel Hous, Hye Way to the, in Hazlitt's Poetry of England . 20
Squyr of Lowe Degre, in Hazlitt's Poetry of England . . . 20
Stanley, T., Predictions, etc., in Aubrey's Miscellanies . . . 8
Stans Puer ad Mensam, in Hazlitt's Poetry of England . . . 20
Style, English, in Ascham's Toxophilus 7
Suckling, Sir John, admiration for Shakespeare. . . . 36
Aglaura, in his Poems, etc. . 36
borrowings from Shakespeare and Balzac's Letters . 36, 37
Brennoralt, first published as the Discontented Colonel, by . 36
Carew criticised by, in his Session of the Poets . . . 11
character and habits of . . 36
comments on his own folly in A Session of the Poets . . 36
Coppy of a Letter Found at Whitehall, by . . . 37
Elegie vpon the Death of Sir Iohn Sutlin 37
Four Fugitives Meeting . . 37
Goblins, The, unfinished play by 37
Letter sent by Sir Iohn Suckling from France 37
Letters 37

PAGE

Suckling, Sir John, Musarum Deliciæ
ridicules his Aglaura . . 36
Newes from Sir John Sucklin . 37
obnoxious to Parliamentarians . 37
Poems, Plays, and other Re-
mains of 36
Religion, An Account of, by . 38
Sad One, The, unfinished trag-
edy by 38
Session of the Poets, his best
known piece 37
Sucklington Faction, The, a
broadside on . . . 38
Surnames, in Camden's Remains . 9
Sutlin, Sir John, Elegie on (Suck-
ling) 37
Swete Susan, in Hazlitt's Poetry of
Scotland 17
Swinburne, A. C., an admirer of
Chapman 13
Symmie and His Bruther, in Haz-
litt's Poetry of Scotland . . 17
Syr Peny, in Hazlitt's Poetry of Eng-
land 20

TABLE-TALK of Selden . . 34
Tale of Colkelbie Sow, in Hazlitt's
Poetry of Scotland . . 17
of Rauf Coilzear, in Hazlitt's
Poetry of Scotland . . 17
of the Basyn, in Hazlitt's Poetry
of England . . . 20
Tales, Early Metrical, by Laing, in-
cluded in Early Popular Poetry of
Scotland 16
Tate, Nahum, alters King Lear . 40
Injured Love, adaptation of
Webster's White Divel . . 40
Tayis Bank, in Hazlitt's Poetry of
Scotland 17
Teresa, St., Crashaw's poem on, in-
spired second part of Christabel . 14
Terne Wathelyn, Awntyrs off Ar-
thure at the, in Hazlitt's Poetry of
Scotland 17

PAGE

Testament, Colyn Blowbols, in Haz-
litt's Poetry of England . . 20
Thames watermen, cries of the 39, 40
Theobald, Lewis, alters Webster's
Duchess of Malfi into The
Fatal Secret 39
Pope on, in Hearne's Re-
mains 21
Thomas of Ersyldoune, etc., in Haz-
litt's Poetry of Scotland . . 17
Thoreau, H. D., praises Quarles's
Enchiridion 32
Thracian Wonder, by Webster and
Rowley 40
Thrie Tailes of the Thrie Priests of
Peblis, in Hazlitt's Poetry of Scot-
land 17
Thrush and the Nightingale, in Haz-
litt's Poetry of England . . 20
Toland, John, on John Aubrey . 8
Tom Thumb, History of, etc., in Haz-
litt's Poetry of England . 18, 20
Topcliffe, Richard, Anne Bellamy's
conduct with 35
Topography, a new science in Cam-
den's time 10
Totenham, Turnament of, in Haz-
litt's Poetry of England . . 20
Tourneur, Cyril, wrote one of Three
Elegies on the Death of Prince
Henrie 39
Tower of London, Overbury impris-
oned in 31
Toxophilus, the schole of shootinge,
by Ascham 7
Trances, in Mather's Remarkable
Providences 30
Transportation by an Invisible Power,
in Aubrey's Miscellanies . . 8
Treatise of a Galaunt, in Hazlitt's
Poetry of England . . . 20
Treatyse shewing the Pryde and
Abuse of Women, etc. . . 20
Triumphes of the Church, see Dray-
ton's Harmonie . . . 15

Tunes for Wither's Hymns and
Songs of the Church . . . 42
Turnament of Totenham, in Hazlitt's
Poetry of England . . . 20
Turnbull, W. B., Crashaw's Works
edited by 14
Drummond's Poetical Works
edited by 15
Southwell's Poetical Works ed-
ted by 35
Turner, Mrs., the poisoner, executed 31
Tyburn, Southwell hanged at . . 35
Tyburn tree and the cry of " West-
" ward Hoe" 40

Unjust Judge, adaptation of
Webster's Appius and Virginia . 38
Urn-Burial, Browne, Sir T., Hydrio-
taphia. 9
Urns, Brampton, by Sir T. Browne . 9
Ussher, Elizabeth, Quarles's Enchi-
ridion dedicated to . . . 32

Verses from Chester's Loves
Martyr, by Marston . . . 28
Virgil, Georgics of, suggested by
Hesiod's Works 12
Virginia, Appius and, by Webster . 38
Vision and Creed of Piers Plough-
man, by Langland . . 22, 23
Visions in a Beryl, in Aubrey's Mis-
cellanies 8
without a Glass, in Aubrey's
Miscellanies 8
Voices, in Aubrey's Miscellanies . 8
Vox and the Wolf, in Hazlitt's Poe-
try of England 20
Vox Populi Vox Dei, in Hazlitt's
Poetry of England . . . 20

Wales, Henry, Prince of, see
Webster's Monumental Columne . 39
Waller, Edmund, praise of Chap-
man's translations . . . 13

Waller, Miss Emma, plays the
" Duchess" in Webster's Duchess
of Malfi 39
Walpole, Horace, Earl of Orford,
on Duchess of Newcastle and her
Works 31
Warning for Faire Women not by
Lilly 23
Warton, Thomas, Sandys's poetry
eulogized by 34
succeeded at Oxford by Spence 35
Warwick, Rev. Arthur, Spare Min-
utes, by 34
Weakest goeth to the VVall, by Web-
ster 40
Webster, John, Appius and Virginia,
a Tragedy, by . . . 38
Cure for a Cuckold, by Rowley
and 38
Deuils Law-case, by . . . 39
Dramatic Works, edited by
Hazlitt 38
Fatal Secret, alteration by Theo-
bald of his Dutchesse of
Malfy 39
Injured Love, a reprint by Tate
of The White Divel . . 40
majority of pieces written in col-
laboration 38
Malcontent, Induction to The,
by 39
Malfy, Tragedy of the Dutchesse
of, by 39
acted in 1850, etc. . . 39
Monumental Columne to Henry,
Prince of Wales . . . 39
Monuments of Honor, by . 39
North-VVard Hoe, by Decker
and 39
Odes, by 39
Thracian Wonder, by Rowley
and 40
Unjust Judge, adaptation of his
Appius 38
Weakest goeth to the VVall, by . 40

INDEX

Webster, John, VVest-VVard Hoe,
by Decker and . . . 40
White Divel, The, by . . 40
Wyat, Famous History of Sir
Thomas, by 40
Webster, William, probable author
of the Thracian Wonder . . 40
Welch Traveller, The, in Hazlitt's
Poetry of England . . . 20
Welcum to May, in Hazlitt's Poetry
of Scotland 17
West, R. W. Sackville-, Sackville's
Works edited by 32
Westminster School, Grant head-
master of 6
VVest-VVard Hoe, by Decker and
Webster 40
cry of the Thames watermen . 40
What You Will, by Marston . . 29
Whipping Stories, in Hearne's Re-
mains 21
White Divel, The, by Webster . 40
White Hall, Carew's Cœlum Britan-
nicum performed at . . . 11
Whitehall, Coppy of a Letter found
at, by Suckling 37
Widow, Hymn for a Widower or a,
in Wither's Hallelujah . . . 41
Wife, by Overbury 32
William of Clowdeslè, in Hazlitt's
Poetry of Scotland . . . 17
Windebank, Sir Francis, see Suck-
ling, Four Fugitives Meeting . 37
Witchcraft in New England and the
two Mathers . . . 29, 30
Witches, Further Account of the
Tryals of the New-England,
by Increase Mather . . 29
Tryals of, in Cotton Mather's
Wonders of the Invisible
World 29
Wither, George, articles on, in Re-
trospective Review . . 42
Denham saves him from hang-
ing 42

Wither, George, described in Pope's
"Dunciad" 41
fought for both Charles I. and
Cromwell 41
Hallelujah; or, Britain's Second
Remembrancer, by . . 40
Hymns and Songs of the Church,
by 41
name spelt also Wyther and
Withers 41
praised by various writers . . 41
published 112 books . . . 41
said to be "Castruccio" in Dav-
enant's Cruel Brother . . 41
tunes for his Hymns of the
Church composed by Gib-
bons 42
Withers, George, see Wither.
W. K., initials used by Marston . 28
Woman in the Moone, by Lilly . 24
Women, a Glasse to viewe the Pride
of Vaine Glorious . . . 20
and marriage, Sir T. Browne's
views on 9
Now a Dayes, A Treatyse shew-
ing Pryde of 20
Schole-house of, in Hazlitt's
Poetry of England . . 20
Wonder of Women, by Marston . 29
Wonders of the Invisible World, by
Mather 29
Wood, Anthony, a friend of John
Aubrey 7
Worde, Wynkyn de, editions of Mal-
ory's Mort d'Arthur by . . 25, 26
Wordsworth, William, praises With-
er's writings 41
Wormius, Hearne as, in Pope's Dun-
ciad 21
Wowing of Jok and Jynny, in Haz-
litt's Poetry of Scotland . . 17
Wright, Thomas, Malory's Mort d'Ar-
thure, edited by . . . 25
Vision and Creed of Piers
Ploughman, edited by . . 22

INDEX

PAGE

Wyat, Sir Thomas, Famous History of, by Webster 40

Wycliffe, John, opinions approved by writer of Creed of Piers Ploughman 22

Wyff, Dumb, maid to Speik, in Hazlitt's Poetry of Scotland . . 18

PAGE

Wyf of Auchtermuchty, in Hazlitt's Poetry of Scotland . . . 18

Wyllyam of Cloudeslè, in Hazlitt's Poetry of England . . . 20

Wynkyn de Worde, *see* Worde.

Wyther, George, *see* Wither.

www.ingramcontent.com/pod-product-compliance
Lightning Source LLC
Chambersburg PA
CBHW020244090426
42735CB00010B/1830